THE GREATEST COUNSELOR
IN THE WORLD

*see Rhema (Gr.) a particular
p. 161 word of the divine word
that we are to use.*

The Greatest Counselor in the World

A Fresh, New Look at the Holy Spirit

Lloyd Ogilvie

Servant Publications
Ann Arbor, Michigan

Copyright © 1995 by Lloyd John Ogilvie
All rights reserved.

Vine Books is an imprint of Servant Publications especially
designed to serve evangelical Christians.

Unless otherwise noted, Scripture passages used in this work are
taken from The New King James Bible. Copyright © 1979,
1980, 1982 by Thomas Nelson, Inc., Publishers.
Used by permission.

The names and characterizations in this book drawn from the
author's ministry and counseling experience are usually rendered
pseudonymously and as fictional composites. Any similarity
between the names and characterizations of these individuals and
real people is unintended and purely coincidental.

Published by Servant Publications
P.O. Box 8617
Ann Arbor, Michigan 48107

Cover design by Multnomah Graphics

95 96 97 98   10 9 8 7 6 5 4

Printed in the United States of America
ISBN 0-89283-909-0

Library of Congress Cataloging-in-Publication Data
Ogilvie, Lloyd
    The greatest counselor in the world : a fresh new look at the
Holy Spirit / Lloyd John Ogilvie
        p. cm.
    Includes bibliographical references.
    ISBN 0-89283-817-5
    1. Christian life—1960- 2. Holy Spirit. I. Title.
BV4501.2.03292 1994
248.4—dc20   94-758
                                                    CIP

Contents

Acknowledgments

Profound gratitude is expressed to all those who helped me prepare this book for publication. I'm thankful for the tireless efforts of Gloria Kilian in typing my first draft of handwritten chapters. Her encouragement through several drafts was a great source of inspiration. Linda Bonar assisted with the typing of several chapters and revisions. Her enthusiasm for the project also spurred me on. During the time of completing the manuscript, Valerie Ulrich was my assistant, and helped me manage my various responsibilities in my church, media ministry, and writing. She has been a great cheerleader for the completion of this book. I am indebted to these three wonderful friends without whom this book would not have been finished.

I want to acknowledge with deep appreciation the help of all the staff at Servant Publications. Thanks to Ann Spangler and Beth Feia for their help in shaping the initial concept and title of this book. And David Came, the managing editor, has been a good friend and creative editor in the final steps of preparing the manuscript for publication. His insightful suggestions were very helpful.

I want to express my greatest thanks to the One about Whom this book is written. Wonder Who that is? Press on to the first chapter!

1) The Greatest Counselor in the World

L IFE IS NOT EASY. We only go around once. And for most it's no merry-go-round ride, but a difficult, bumpy journey.

Problems get us down. Minor problems and sometimes serious ones. Many of them never seem to go away. We overcome one obstacle and then get hit by another one with full force. Often problems pile up. Worry about them saps our strength and creativity. They accumulate and suddenly too many surface at the same time. Panic sets in. We wonder how much we can take. We can take one problem if we can concentrate all our energies on solving it. But so often our energies are dissipated by other problems that worsen at the same time. It's difficult to stay up during financial hard times. Our own health problems or those of our loved ones make us anxious. Our carefully laid plans get messed up by human error or carelessness. Foul-ups happen at work, at home. Then, as if staying afloat wasn't difficult enough, we feel the undertow of the larger social problems of violence, racial tensions, and human misery when we turn on the television news.

We keep waiting for a time when all our problems are behind us, so we can really start living. It never comes. The stuff of life involves facing and solving problems—learning and growing through them. Who can help us overcome our seemingly endless list of problems?

OUR URGENT NEED—WHO CAN HELP US?

Many of our biggest problems are wrapped up in people. Often their need for affirmation and encouragement seems insatiable. Some are easily hurt, some are competitive, still others need recognition. We all know the excruciating pain of being misunderstood by those we love or friends we are trying to help.

Communication is one of the key challenges in marriage. A wife said to her husband, "We're passing like ships in the night. You say you understand what you think I'm saying, but what you think you are hearing is not what I'm saying!"

And raising children to be mature adults with self-esteem is an awesome calling. It means riding out the storms of discipline, rebellion, and anguish. Sibling rivalry keeps many families on edge, even after the children are adults.

Even in the best of families, there are tensions when aging parents must be parented by their adult children through the difficult periods of declining health, nursing care, and an ever-increasing need for attention and time.

At work, we can trace most problems back to someone who's the cause. Communication breaks down and so does efficiency. I met an office manager at the end of a stressful day who exclaimed, "People and computers! I'm ready to throw out both!"

Among our friends, we all have people with the, "What have you done for me lately?" attitude. Then there are those who are facing real difficulties and we long to help bear the burdens they are carrying. It would be great if we could meet everyone's needs!

In the church, there are times when fellow Christians get on our nerves. Every church has its share of difficult people who want to be served rather than to serve. There are unmet ego needs at the heart of many squabbles that keep the church from being the beloved community Jesus intended.

We wish we could see beneath the surface of people, understand their insecurities, and know what to say and do. Simply keeping our relationships in order is a full-time job, with overtime required most every day, even many nights. We wonder if we have what it takes to deal with needy, demanding, frustrating people. A lot of the time we're sure we don't have the patience and endurance required. Who can help us find the love we need when we feel like we just don't have any more to give?

～

*I met an office manager at the end of a stressful day
who exclaimed, "People and computers!
I'm ready to throw out both!"*

～

But not all of us are externalizers who readily identify other people as our problems. Some of us are internalizers who feel that our most formidable problems are with the person who lives inside our own skin. The externalizer tends to blame others; the internalizer blames himself or herself. If there is a problem, internalizers usually assume they caused it. A syndrome of low self-esteem, multiplied by memories of failures and mistakes, equals a deep sense of inadequacy.

Internalizers have a very active inner child, to use a term coined by psychology and the recovery movement. The same fears we had as children influence our adult lives. If we sensed as children that love and approval were dependent on our performance, we place similar conditions on ourselves in adulthood. The fears of our growing years become the settled condition of our attitudes toward ourselves. Fears of punishment, rejection, and alienation linger into adulthood.

There are three people living inside of internalizers—the ideal self, the performing self, and the punitive self. The punitive self often dominates by heaping blame for ineptness on the performing self and ridicule for the possibility of ever achieving on the ideal self. A pervading sense of guilt results. Guilt is a feeling of self-judgment. It's conditioned approval of ourselves, our capacity for self-evaluation gone sour. Sometimes it's rooted in specific memories of failure, but more often it's a floating dis-ease caused by dis-grace—uneasiness fostered by a lack of gracious acceptance of ourselves. It's the restless disapproval of ourselves that thrashes about in us looking for tangible evidence of our shortcomings.

~

Internalizers miss a lot of the joy of living. Who can infuse the esteem and confidence needed to stop worrying and start living?

~

A friend of mine who is an internalizer received a call from his boss setting up an appointment to talk over a problem. My friend immediately assumed that he had either caused some problem or was the problem. He spent three anguishing days before the time of the appointment. When he did meet with the boss, he was greatly relieved to learn that the problem was related to a production schedule in the plant where he worked. Concluding the conference, his boss said, "I'm really glad I have a person like you to tackle and solve this problem."

Later my friend said to me, "When I think of all the worry and anxiety of those three days waiting for that appointment, I kick myself around the block for assuming I was the problem!" Notice how quickly my friend shifted from thinking he was the problem to punishing himself for the way he reacted. He was not able to enjoy the affirmation his boss had given him. Instead, he was critical of himself for expecting the worst.

A woman with whom I was having a conversation persisted in giving herself a tongue-lashing for some failures. "You know, I sound just like my mother. I guess I've taken over where she left off." My response was, "Are you always this hard on yourself?" She said, "Well, someone has to keep me in line!"

Then I think of a man who always internalizes problems when they surface in his marriage. His wife says, "I wish he wasn't so quick to blame himself. He says, 'I'm sorry,' before we have a chance to talk out what went wrong. Point of fact, most often we're both to blame, but we never get to the real issue. He runs for cover by assuming the guilt and escapes any real responsibility for working out a solution."

Internalizers miss a lot of the joy of living. Who can infuse the esteem and confidence needed to stop worrying and start living?

Decisions stare all of us in the face as well. Seemingly insignificant daily decisions about the expenditure of our time, energy, and money can have long-range implications. Crossroad decisions about our careers, crucial moves, and lifestyle choices force us to think about where we are headed and the quality of person we want to be. Moral and social issues test our integrity. We struggle to clarify our goals distracted by a cacophony of voices suggesting a thousand different directions. Some previous decisions soberly remind us that the margin of error is high. The risks make us very cautious. Sometimes we get bogged down and muddle through life, deciding not to decide but then paying the consequences. We long to have 20/20 hindsight to learn from the past. Most of all, we wish we had better discernment about what's best for our lives and for those for whom we are responsible, especially loved ones in our care. We yearn to have someone share the burden with us and lead us to make the right decisions. But who has enough wisdom to do that? Whom can we trust?

❧

When life doesn't turn out the way we've planned, we tend to get discouraged and angry. When the anger builds up inside, we feel depressed and are not sure what to do about it.

❧

Along with people problems and tough decisions, life also dishes out disappointments. Little ones hassle our daily happiness and peace of mind. Big ones hamper our long-range hopes for the future.

In one week recently, I talked to people who represented the broad spectrum of human disappointments. A man expressed his anguish at being bypassed for a position he'd worked hard to be awarded. Only two people at the office disagreed with his assessment: the boss and his fellow employee who got the promotion. A woman battled with disappointment over her two children who, as yet, shared neither her beliefs nor her values. A man expressed his exasperation over his son who turned down the opportunity to follow in his footsteps and take over the family business. An actress who had achieved some measure of fame and success confessed her disappointment that she had not had a chance to work for several years. A man who also is out of work shared his growing anxiety and diminished self-esteem. People who had debilitating illnesses talked about their disappointment over their physical limitations. A woman sobbed out the pain over her broken relationship with her husband.

"Quite a week!" you say. And yet, people are enduring disappointments all around us. The Scottish poet Robert Burns was right, "If each man's internal care were written on his brow, those who have our envy, would have our pity now." All of us, at times, are disappointed.

When life doesn't turn out the way we've planned, we tend to get discouraged and angry. When the anger builds up inside, we feel depressed and are not sure what to do about it. Where can we turn to receive comfort and counsel in our hour of trial?

Even in the midst of a busy life surrounded by people, often we feel quite lonely. Does anyone really care about *me*? We are anxious about trying to do the best we can with what we have and receiving recognition for it. Fear of failure often racks us, especially when we face new challenges and responsibilities at work and at home. An even greater fear of rejection keeps our exterior highly polished, while—at the same time—we hide what's really going on inside. Can we trust anyone to understand our deepest fears and insecurities?

~

We need someone to listen and understand—someone who will allow us to talk until we know what we are trying to say.

~

All of this can happen to good people, religious people, church people, who discover that life is difficult. There's an aching need for strength, courage, and confidence. Inner certainty and serenity are lacking. Religion begins to wear thin. Vibrant hope starts to dim. Something important is missing. But to whom shall we go to find the missing piece of the puzzle?

We need someone to listen and understand—someone who will allow us to talk until we know what we are trying to say. And we need someone who will probe to the nub of the issue, who has the authority and wisdom to help us see any confusion in our thinking or distortions in our emotions. This someone not only needs to lead us to the truth about our-selves and our lives, but also must possess the strength to empower us to act on what we know we must do and be. Above all, we need someone who has the power to heal our painful memories, sharpen our vision of what is best for our future, and catch us up in a purpose beyond ourselves—one that's big enough to fire our imaginations and give ultimate meaning and lasting joy to daily living.

That's a tall order. No friend, psychiatrist, psychologist, pas-tor, or spiritual advisor can meet all of these qualifications. But they may help lead us to the One Who has all these gifts. He alone has the omniscience, omnipresence, and omnipotence to be the kind of counselor we need. He can help us with our problems, relationships, and decisions for He knows every-thing. He is with us always, for He never sleeps. He has all power to give us strength and courage, for He is the Holy Spirit with us and wants to live within us.

THE GREATEST COUNSELOR IN THE WORLD

The Holy Spirit is the greatest Counselor in the world. The word "counselor" may not be the first word that comes to your mind when you think of the Holy Spirit. For many, the Holy Spirit is the least known and understood Person of the Trinity. For others, He is associated almost exclusively with Pentecost, the gift of tongues, or the charismatic church. And for some, the Holy Spirit is the subject of dispute about when He is received, what is the evidence of His presence in the life of a Christian, and customs that have emerged to celebrate His presence in contemporary worship in some churches.

But to a growing number of Christians around the world today, the Holy Spirit is known and praised by the name Jesus used to declare what the Spirit would be in the lives of His disciples after Pentecost. The Greek word is *Paraklētos*, a cornucopian word overflowing with inspiring implications. It is translated as *Comforter* in the King James, *Helper* in the New King James, and *Counselor* in the Revised Standard Version and the New International Version.

We can appreciate more fully the ministry of the Holy Spirit as our Counselor when we understand the use of this propitious name *Parakletos.* The Greek word is rich in meaning. It was associated with courts of law and signifies one who is the counsel for the defense, one who pleads on behalf of another. In a broader sense, it identifies one who stands by a person's side or one who is ready to aid a soldier in battle.

∾

"And I will ask the Father, and He will give you
another Counselor to be with
you forever—the Spirit of truth.... He lives
with you and will be in you." John 14:16-17, NIV

∾

Now consider how the word was used for Christ Himself. The apostle John writes, "We have an Advocate (*Parakletos*) with the Father, Jesus Christ the righteous. And He Himself is the propitiation (*hilasmos*—the means whereby sin is remitted) for our sins, and not for ours only but also for the whole world" (1 John 2:1-2). John knew this to be true from Jesus' own self-identification to the disciples, then in the apostle's personal witness of the death of Christ, and, most of all, in his own experience of the risen Lord through the Holy Spirit. Christ pleads our case before the Father on the basis of His sacrifice on the cross. When we believe in Christ and His atoning death for us, He is our Advocate before the Father, claiming the same love for us as the Father has for Him. Incredible!

In that light, next consider Christ's words about the Holy Spirit spoken in the Upper Room on the night before He was crucified. He promised *another* Advocate. "And I will ask the

Father, and He will give you another Counselor to be with you forever—the Spirit of truth.... He lives with you and will be in you" (John 14:16-17, NIV). The word "another" needs underlining. The Greek word used is *allos,* another of the same kind, not *heteros,* meaning another of a different kind. Then Jesus went on with this mind-stretching promise, "I will not leave you orphans; I will come to you" and further, "At that day you will know that I am in My Father and you in Me and I in you" (John 14:18, 20).

In light of the unity of the Persons of the Trinity, we can press on to understand and experience the particular ministry of the Holy Spirit as our Counselor in the stresses and strains as well as the opportunities and challenges of daily living.

WHAT A DIFFERENCE THE SPIRIT MAKES

Allow me to share my own experience of the Spirit as Counselor. It began many years ago while I was a post-graduate student at the University of Edinburgh. I had lived a few years as a Christian with firm trust in Christ as my Lord and Savior before I realized the power to live the Christian life. I did my best to be an orthodox believer with evangelical fervor. Seldom a day passed without Bible study and prayer. I shared my faith and tried to be a faithful disciple. With a crusader's zeal, I entered into battles for social justice.

∾

Keeping up the image of victorious Christian living became very exhausting, particularly when I failed. A pervading tension inside finally brought me to the breaking point.

∾

The problem, however, was that I was trying to live for Christ rather than empowered by Him through the Holy

Spirit. My problem was pride: I wanted to be a good Christian on my own steam. This led to a dishonest duality: I was a polished Christian on the outside; inside I felt empty, unsure, and insecure. And I tried all the harder to keep the exterior shining bright, so no one else would know. That came across to others as arrogance or, at the very least, pretentious piety.

Needing to be right, I defended my decisions with stubbornness. Insecure, I became all the more determined to control my life and the people around me. That brought tensions in my marriage. I'll never forget the day my wife, Mary Jane, said, "Lloyd, you're trying so hard. You talk about love more than anyone I know, but I don't feel love from you."

In sharing my faith, so often I had the words without the music. The biblical orthodoxy was there, but seldom was there a personal illustration of what the Gospel was doing for me. My least favorite verse was, "We have this treasure in earthen vessels that the excellence of the power may be of God and not of us" (2 Corinthians 4:7). I wanted to hold the treasure in a silver vessel, excellent in my pure theology and what I thought was exemplary discipleship.

Keeping up the image of victorious Christian living became very exhausting, particularly when I failed. A pervading tension inside finally brought me to the breaking point. I searched the message of Christ in the New Testament for an answer, all the while crying out, "Lord, help me!"

Alone on a retreat, I felt led to John, chapters 14 through 16, about the promise of the Holy Spirit. Paul's word to the Ephesians, "Be filled with the Spirit" (Ephesians 5:18), resounded in my mind as well. In the long hours of silence, the Lord seemed to keep saying, "Lloyd, the Holy Spirit led you to Me, now let Me lead you to the Holy Spirit. You're adrift. Lift the sails of your mind and heart. Let Me fill them with the wind of the Spirit. You need daily power, guidance, wisdom, and vision. Most of all, you need to allow Me to love you, to heal the insecurities from childhood and the memories of past failures. Stop trying to control Me. Instead, let Me control you. Don't be afraid of losing Me by being filled constantly with the Holy Spirit. We are one! In being filled with Him, you will know Me better than ever before. The energy you've squandered on trying to be adequate, He will multiply beyond your imagination, so you can glorify and serve Me."

The Lord had put His finger on a raw nerve. My pride, yes, but something more. In my passion to be a disciple, I feared that opening myself to the Holy Spirit was somehow disloyalty to Christ. My faith was rooted in the historical Christ, His death and victorious resurrection alone. With everything within me, I had tried to serve the risen, reigning Christ. That was the problem. Everything within me had run out. My tank was running on empty.

~

*"It is to your advantage that I go away; for if
I do not go away, the Helper (Counselor)
will not come to you; but if I depart, I will
send Him to you."* John 16:7

~

So there I sat during my solitary retreat feeling the same emotions of panic experienced by the disciples in the Upper Room after the crucifixion and resurrection, but before Pentecost. Like them, the Master's words, "It is to your advantage that I go away; for if I do not go away, the Helper (Counselor) will not come to you; but if I depart, I will send Him to you" (John 16:7), were discomforting. Yet, as I pondered their meaning, I realized that was exactly what was happening to me. Christ was saying that He was pulling me away from my limited stage of growth, so He could pull me on to a new and exciting experience of Himself though the power of the Holy Spirit. Words I'd read in G. Campbell Morgan's commentary on Acts came thundering to mind with reassuring force: "Thirty minutes after Pentecost, the disciples knew more of Christ than they had learned through three years of following Him as Jesus of Nazareth."[1] Was that true? I wondered. I felt gripped by the desire to find out for myself.

I got down on my knees. "Lord Jesus," I prayed, "I know I could not have believed in You without the gift of faith from the Holy Spirit. But, since then, I've given little thought to the Holy Spirit. Now You have shown me that You and He are one, through Him You can live in me. He will empower me to serve You. I confess that I've feared losing control. That's absurd. I've already lost control trying to be Your disciple on my own energy.

"With the same earnestness that I confessed my faith in You, Christ, I confess my trust in, and need for, the Holy Spirit. I ask to be filled with the Holy Spirit and make a covenant to keep allowing Him to fill me. Lord, as the Holy Spirit led me to You, now lead me to Him so I can glorify You and serve You with authentic power and not my limited and now depleted strength. Lord, I need the Holy Spirit, I want the Holy Spirit, I yield myself to the Holy Spirit."

While still on my knees, I felt a palpable surge of power throbbing in my body. A warmth flooded my whole being. A sense of peace, security, and well-being invaded my turbulent heart and mind. I felt loved and cherished. Then an indomitable will to press on captured my own will. I was ready to live again, really for the first time.

The difference this experience made in my life, marriage, and ministry was startling, first to me, and then to those around me. Morgan was right: the Holy Spirit did free me to know, love, and serve Christ better than ever before!

THE NEXT STEP

I have shared this account because it was a prelude to a next step I was led to take about a year later. This step is directly germane to the thrust of this book.

In my continued quest to know the Holy Spirit better, I kept coming back to this word, *Paraklētos*. I began a daily experiment of claiming Him as my Counselor. I had been through clinical training in counseling and knew what a human counselor should do. I had learned listening skills, how to draw a person out, and how to communicate unqualified acceptance. It hit me that this was exactly what the Holy Spirit did for me in an infinitely deeper way when I gave Him a chance by being completely honest with Him—allowing Him to lead me to deeper truth about myself and my thoughts and feelings.

Often when I remained in silent listening prayer, insights came to me that were so far beyond my own understanding that I was simply amazed. Sometimes when I was stressed out, feeling jangled emotionally, quiet listening revealed a deeper cause that I would not have discovered on my own. When I asked for help with strained or broken relationships, often I was shown more than I wanted to admit about what I had done or said to cause the problems. Added to that, it was revealed to me what I had to do or say as my part in bringing healing.

∽

Often in the silence of prayer the Holy Spirit gave me empathy, love, and discernment I could not have produced myself.

∽

Intercessory prayer took on a whole different focus. I came to my Counselor with the needs of people and confessed I didn't know what was best or how to pray. Often in the silence of prayer the Holy Spirit gave me empathy, love, and discernment I could not have produced myself. It was astounding—I was given many times a kind of X-ray penetration into what was really going on inside people.

The same thing began to happen in my prayer for specific situations, problems, and decisions. In my quiet time with my Counselor, the Holy Spirit, I started the practice of talking out what was confronting me. Slowly, but persistently, I was taught to leave my concerns with Him in a complete surrender. Sometimes the answer came quickly; other times I had to wait in patient trust. With His power, I was able to press on to do what He had convinced me was best, would glorify Christ, and bring His ultimate good to everyone concerned. In it all, I discovered that if I made a less than creative decision or really goofed things up, I could ask for and receive forgiveness. But better than that, I learned that if I admitted my mistakes, the Holy Spirit would bring some good out of them that I never could have foreseen.

I have recounted my fledgling beginning years ago as a counselee of the Holy Spirit. The relationship grows deeper every day, especially as I try to put down in writing what He means to me.

THE FATHER'S OUTSTRETCHED ARMS

I am stunned by the magnificent way the three Persons of the Trinity work together. Irenaeus, church father of the second century, has given us an apt image for this unity. Picture the Father reaching out with two arms. One is Christ through Whom He reached out to redeem the world and now reaches us with the power of the cross. The other arm is the Holy Spirit Who works in us, convincing us of Christ's atoning death and our forgiveness, giving us the gift of faith to respond. With the two arms the Father draws us to His heart. Both arms are crucial. Without the arm of the Holy Spirit, it is impossible for us to appropriate what the arm of Christ has done and does for us.

This image is helpful because it avoids tri-theism, three

gods. All three Persons of the Trinity work, not in tandem (one after the other), but in triune interaction. All three were involved in creation, throughout the Old Testament, and sublimely in the Incarnation. The Father sent the Son. The Son humbled Himself in obedience (Philippians 2:6), was conceived in the Virgin Mary by the miracle of the Holy Spirit, was born in Bethlehem, and lived as the Son of God and Son of Man with the perfect balance of the divine and the human in His nature. With the power of the Holy Spirit at work in and around Him, Christ healed the sick, performed miracles, and revealed God as He is and what we were meant to be.

Keeping in mind that Father, Son, and Holy Spirit are one, allow your mind and heart to soar while reflecting on the mutual submission between them. Jesus was obedient to the Father and dependent in the flesh upon the power of the Holy Spirit. His single purpose was to glorify the Father.

After His atoning death on the cross, the Father raised Him up, glorified Him, and gave Him the name of Yahweh, Lord, His own Name, the Name above all names (Philippians 2:9-11). *And* He gave to the reigning Lord the authority to pour out the power of the Holy Spirit. Peter witnessed to this at Pentecost: "Therefore being exalted at the right hand of God, and having received from the Father the promise of the Holy Spirit, He poured out this which you now see and hear" (Acts 2:33).

∼

Keeping in mind that Father, Son, and Holy Spirit are one,
allow your mind and heart to soar while reflecting on the
mutual submission between them.

∼

My esteemed professor, Dr. Thomas F. Torrance, who taught me how to keep my thinking clear about the Trinity, helps us understand how Christ and the Holy Spirit work together in our lives today:

The Spirit is so intimately one with Christ in His being and activity as the incarnate Son of God that He is, as it were, Christ's *Other Self,* through whose presence in us Christ is present to us. The Spirit seals our adoption in Christ as children of God and unites us to Christ in such a way that we are made by grace to share in His filial relation to the Father. The Holy Spirit is the living and life-giving Spirit of God who actualizes the self-giving of God to us in His Son, and resonates and makes fruitful within us the priestly, atoning and intercessory activity of Christ on our behalf.... It is through the incarnation and atonement effected by the conjoint activity of Christ and the Holy Spirit that God has opened the door for us to enter into His holy presence and know Him as He really is in Himself in His triune being. In this two way movement of atoning propitiation whereby God draws near to us and draws us near to Himself, the access to the Father given to us through the grace of the Lord Jesus Christ and in the communion of the Holy Spirit is such that we are enabled, quite astonishingly and beyond any worth or capacity of our own, to participate, creaturely beings though we are, in the eternal communion and inner relations of knowing and loving within God Himself, and know Him there as one God in three Persons, Father, Son, and Holy Spirit.[2]

The ministry of the Holy Spirit in this period between Pentecost and the second coming of Christ and the end of human history is to glorify Christ. Christ Himself described how the Holy Spirit would do this. His words are recorded for us in John, chapter 16, and in His prayer in John 17. Working in complete harmony with the risen, reigning Christ, the Holy Spirit functions as the greatest Counselor in the world in the marvelous ways Jesus promised:

1. He is the Spirit of Truth who enables us to know the truth about ourselves and the truth of Christ.

2. He will teach us all things and bring to our remembrance all that Christ said and did.

3. He will convict us of sin and judgment and then assure us of our righteousness through Christ's atonement.

4. He will guide us.

5. He will take all that the Father has given to Christ and declare it to us.

6. He will be the Sanctifier, enabling our growth in holiness, the awesome miracle of making us in Christ's likeness.

7. Through the Holy Spirit the risen Christ makes Himself known to us and dwells in us.

MEANWHILE, BACK TO THE ASPHALT JUNGLE

Now we can see why the Holy Spirit is qualified to be our Counselor in the problems, decisions, people-pressures, disappointments, struggles, and loneliness we experience in the asphalt jungle of today's modern world. His assignment is to work in us as our Counselor, to change and guide our thinking, show us the way, and be sure we arrive safely in heaven at the end of our physical life.

∼

Remember Christ promised that He and the Father would make their home in us. He also promised that the Counselor would live in us.

∼

Through the Holy Spirit, we are included in the loop of what I like to call the glory circle. At any one moment in time, right now as you are reading this, the Father is glorifying the Son as the only way to His heart; the Son lives to glorify the Father by constantly seeking to reconcile all things, you and me, to Him; the Holy Spirit glorifies the Son and the Father by dwelling in us, giving us the power to obey the Father and the faith to trust in the Son. Since our chief end is to glorify God and enjoy Him forever, the counseling ministry of the Holy Spirit is to keep us in the loop with everything we do and say being a glorification of the Father and the Son through Him.

Remember Christ promised that He and the Father would make their home in us. He also promised that the Counselor would live in us. We really get it all together—or more precisely, the subsistencies of God together—when we willingly yield to being drawn into the interaction of Father, Son, and Holy Spirit in the glory circle. We have the security of the Father's authority with His ultimate demands for holiness, righteousness, and justice constantly before us. At the same time, we have Christ our Lord interceding for us, claiming His righteousness for us. And we have the Holy Spirit advising, warning, alerting, and empowering us.

TWO-THIRDS IS NOT ENOUGH

Sadly, many Christians settle for two-thirds of God. God the Father is way up there somewhere, aloof and apart from their daily lives. Christ is out there, somewhere between them and the Father. The Holy Spirit is some kind of vague force or impersonal power they hear about but do not know intimately. The greatest misconception of all is that we, on our own, conjured up faith in God and in Christ's atonement. We overlook the clear biblical assertion that "no one can say that Jesus Christ is Lord except by the Holy Spirit" (1 Corinthians 12:3). The truth is that the Holy Spirit creates in us our attraction to Christ. He engenders the gift of faith. He instigates our conversion, and He enables us to take our first steps in the Christian life.

The Holy Spirit is gracious, unintrusive, and patient. His purpose is not to glorify Himself but to glorify Christ. Some people whose introduction to the Christian life included clear teaching about the power of the Holy Spirit, welcome Him and His counseling ministry as part of their initial conversion.

Others make their commitment to Christ and press on trying to be a Christian on their own strength and sagacity. Later on, often much later on, they realize they are attempting an impossibility. The Christian life becomes a cycle of brave attempts and sad failures. They feel defeated, impotent, and frustrated. When a big crisis hits, they suddenly realize that they don't have what it takes and cry out for help.

~

This experience of submitting to the greatest Counselor in the world has been described with various terms. Some call it the baptism of the Holy Spirit, others refer to it as the second blessing, and others describe it as being filled with the Holy Spirit.

~

Often this is the sublime moment when Christians are open to learn about the empowering, counseling ministry of the Holy Spirit for the first time. They then welcome in the One Who has been waiting to be their Helper, Comforter, and Counselor. These Christians experience immense relief that they no longer need to run their own lives through sheer will power. Their joy is uncontainable because they experience grace as a vital, healing reality, not as a theory. Their new-found security and assurance in God are unshakable. These Christians have claimed the power of the Holy Spirit that was theirs all along but remained untapped.

This experience of submitting to the greatest Counselor in the world has been described with various terms. Some call it the baptism of the Holy Spirit, others refer to it as the second blessing, and others describe it as being filled with the Holy Spirit. I prefer the latter. For me, it most clearly describes what happens when we yield the control of our lives to the Spirit. When we accept the controlling power of the Spirit, we realize the resources that were always ours but never claimed.

And that's only the beginning. In the Greek there is a tense called the present passive imperative. Paul uses it in a key verse, Ephesians 5:18, which I mentioned earlier. In our English Bibles the words appear, "Be filled with the Holy Spirit." It sounds like Paul is calling the Ephesian Christians to a new experience. Not so. They had received the Holy Spirit and had been sealed with His assurance (Ephesians 1:13). The correct translation of "Be filled with the Holy Spirit" should be: "Keep on allowing the Holy Spirit to fill you." It's an ever-present *now* experience; it is done to us rather than by us; it is an imperative command to yield. Every day, every hour, each moment, the secret of supernatural power is to keep on allowing the Holy Spirit to fill us. Or, in the context of this book, at all times keep open to the guidance, wisdom, and power of the greatest Counselor.

∽

"The wind blows where it wishes and you do not know where it comes from and where it goes. So is everyone born of the Spirit." John 3:8

∽

This book is being written in a little apartment in the Highlands of Scotland. It's now many years since my first experience of submitting my life to the Holy Spirit as my Counselor.

As I sit here looking out at the magnificent mountains, I think of the words of the psalmist: "I will lift up my eyes to the hills—from whence comes my help? My help comes from the Lord who made heaven and earth" (Psalm 121:1-2). I feel that same confidence. But God is not only my Creator, He's my Redeemer in Christ, my Lord, and my Sustainer in the

Holy Spirit. I reflect on the confidence the Holy Spirit has given me. It's so much more than self-confidence.

Outside the winds are blowing. The summer is over and the smell of fall is in the air. Every so often the strong gusts of the wind rattle the window in front of the desk where I'm working. Where did that wind come from? Where is it going? I hear the whirring sound of it and see it sweep across the countryside, swaying the trees with its velocity.

Little wonder the Hebrew word for wind is *ruach*. The guttural pronunciation of the word has the sound of rushing wind. The word in Hebrew was used for the breath of life. *Ruach* is also the word for the Spirit of God—His supernatural power that takes possession of the lives of people and gives them indomitable confidence in the Father's love and the grace of the Lord Jesus Christ.

As I listen to the wind roar and watch it blow away the heavy, dark clouds that have hung over the mountains for days, I remember Jesus' words to Nicodemus that certainly have been my experience, "The wind blows where it wishes and you do not know where it comes from and where it goes. So is everyone born of the Spirit" (John 3:8).

~

The embers of my faith receive a bellows-blessing and are revived again: first a flickering flame, then a white hot fire in the hearth of my heart. The Holy Spirit has gotten my attention again, as He does every day.

~

Now as I look back over the years, I'm profoundly thankful that when I was most lacking in strength and courage, the Holy Spirit found the boat of my life, drifting with the currents of the day. He filled the sails of my soul and got me moving. Little did I know then where He would take me, the authentic confidence in His power He would give me, and the freedom from fear and anxiety He would provide me. Just thinking about that, I sense the fresh winds of the Holy Spirit stirring, gusting, and then blowing with mighty force inside my own spirit.

Another metonym for the Spirit in the Scriptures is fire. John the Baptist prophesied that Christ would baptize us with the Holy Spirit and fire (Luke 3:16). I'm reminded of that as the wind I've seen blowing outside my window now also gusts down the chimney, reviving the low burning embers in the fireplace across the room. The Holy Spirit set a fire in the hearth of my heart long ago and bellows it into flame daily. He gives the fire of conviction, burns out the chaff, and constantly renews my passion to serve Christ. The embers of my faith receive a bellows-blessing and are revived again: first a flickering flame, then a white hot fire in the hearth of my heart. The Holy Spirit has gotten my attention again, as He does every day. He calls me into a counseling session with Him as my Counselor.

◆

But before you turn the page, pause to reflect on your own experience and relationship with the Holy Spirit. Have you ever intentionally spent time alone with Him as your Counselor? Try it right now.

◆

In the chapters of this book, I want to share what the adventure of being a counselee of the Holy Spirit can mean in our lives. We'll discover: how He helps us know God's will; how to love and glorify Christ; how to overcome our biggest difficulties; how to deal with times when we don't know how or what to pray or even what to pray for; how to receive refreshing drafts of faith, hope, and love each day; how to handle our yesterdays; how to survive in spiritual warfare; and how to press on with supernatural power.

But before you turn the page, pause to reflect on your own experience and relationship with the Holy Spirit. Have you ever intentionally spent time alone with Him as your Counselor? Try it right now.

Begin by asking Him to give you a fresh infilling of His power, wisdom, peace, and joy. Then talk to Him about the deepest need you are feeling right at this moment. Now be quiet and listen for His response.

The assignment of the Holy Spirit as the Third Person of the Trinity is to be your Counselor and mine. And when we trust Him, we discover He's the greatest counselor in the world!

2 ⟩ Sealed by the Holy Spirit

I STUDIED WITH INTENSE INTEREST the wax seal on an old document. It was the seal of a Highland Scots clan. The clan crest and motto were clearly discernible in the impression in the wax. My excitement grew as I read the motto, "A Fin," meaning, "To the end." The seal was of the Ogilvie clan!

In a real way that seal has been pressed into my own heart. Over the years, Ogilvie clan history and memorabilia have been one of my hobbies. I inherited my appreciation of my heritage from my father and have tried to pass it on to my children and grandchildren. My sons and I wear gold rings all alike with the Ogilvie seal etched on them, exactly the same as the seal on that document. This crest seal gives us a bonding with history and with each other.

And so the Ogilvie heritage is passed on from generation to generation dating back to 1163 when William the Lion granted the Barony of Ogilvie to Gilbert, a descendent of the ancient Earls of Angus. Finding that old document with the Ogilvie

Ogilvie seal on it stirred my commitment to live by our motto, "To the end." An explanation of the motto by a crusty old clan kinsman I met years ago often comes to mind and challenges me to attempt my best. "The Ogilvies fight to the end," he said with the thick burr. "We never give up; we see things through!"

A FAR GREATER SEAL

As important as the impression of the Ogilvie seal has been in my life, it is nothing in comparison to another infinitely more transforming seal that has been pressed into my soul. This seal gives me eternal security and assurance: "Nevertheless, the solid foundation of God stands, *having this seal,* 'The Lord knows those who are His,' and 'Let everyone who names the name of Christ depart from iniquity'" (2 Timothy 2:19, emphasis mine).

◠

Talk about heritage and belonging! Our security dates back beyond history to eternity. God chose us to be part of His family before history began.

◠

This seal of the family of God means everything to me. It roots me not only in history, but in eternity. The more I study it, the more security I feel in the privilege of belonging to God.

Consider the first part of the Lord's seal. The words "The Lord knows" should read, "The Lord knew." *Egnō*—the timeless, eternal, aorist perfect of *gignōskō*—is used in the original Greek. This means the Lord *knew* us and had plans for us even before time and creation. In fact, the Incarnation and Christ's transforming redemption were planned with you and me in mind. Think of it! God had a plan for you before the stars were hung and the planet Earth was set revolving around the sun. All this so that, by the Father's divine election, we might be chosen, "According to His own purpose and grace which was given to us in Christ Jesus *before time began*" (2 Timothy 1:9, emphasis mine).

Talk about heritage and belonging! Our security dates back beyond history to eternity. God chose us to be part of His family before history began. He predetermined that we should be His sons and daughters. Awesome! His choice was not based on our achievement since we had not yet been born. Thousands of light years after His choice of us, we chose to claim our election. We chose to accept our chosenness; we claimed our place in the family of God through Christ because He had already claimed us. Pride is engulfed by praise. "You have not chosen me," Christ reminds us, "but I have chosen you" (John 15:16).

Now consider the second part of the seal of God: "Let everyone who names the name of Christ depart from iniquity." The Greek word for "depart" is *apostētō*, to stand aloof or apart. The word for "iniquity" is *adikia*, unrighteousness. Put in a positive sense, we have been chosen and called to live righteous lives. We have been elected to be elevated into a right relationship with God through Christ's reconciling death and resurrection. We become the righteousness of God (2 Corinthians 5:21). We decide to be chosen and claim our new family likeness with Christ.

THE SEALING OF THE HOLY SPIRIT

I will go into the meaning of the various aspects of the seal later in this chapter, but before I do that we need to think about the One Who does the sealing.

The Holy Spirit, our Counselor, is the sealing agent of God. It is His responsibility to impress the two parts of the seal of God in our minds and hearts. Both at the beginning of our Christian life and daily through the years until we graduate to heaven, He is there as God's sealing agent. His ministry is to assure us that we belong to God and to guide us into righteous living, that is, to shape us in the image of Christ. Paul calls this the sealing of the Holy Spirit. "In Him [Christ] you also trusted, after you heard the word of truth, the Gospel of your salvation; in Whom also, *having believed,* you were sealed with the Holy Spirit of promise, Who is the guarantee of our inheritance until the redemption of the purchased possession, to the praise of His glory" (Ephesians 1:13-14, brackets and emphasis mine).

~

The Holy Spirit, our Counselor, is the sealing
agent of God. It is His responsibility to impress
the two parts of the seal of God
in our minds and hearts.

~

What is this sealing of the Holy Spirit? We need to be very clear about the metaphor of sealing because it gives us a vivid picture of how the Holy Spirit assumes and continues His work as our Counselor. Allow me to explain briefly.

In New Testament times and throughout history, people have used a seal on an object *to indicate ownership.* Sealing was done by dripping hot wax onto an item and then pressing a person's seal into it. The seal was the crest, name, identifying brand, or initials of the owner. People sealed valued documents (like the clan documents I found), letters, and objects. This practice was common in sending official papers, crates, and packages because they clearly identified the sender. Possessions taken with a person on a trip were sealed to protect them from loss or theft. Seals were used by individuals and families and subsequently by universities, cities, and nations— most often displaying their crest and motto.

∼

In New Testament times and throughout history, people have used a seal on an object to indicate ownership.

∼

Now we're ready to consider the biblical meaning of the sealing of the Holy Spirit. We get a clue to the spiritual meaning from Christ's words about His own sealing. In John 6:27, He said, "Do not labor for the food which perishes, but for the food which endures to everlasting life, which the Son of Man will give you, because God the Father has set His seal on Him." Christ was referring to His baptism. Matthew tells us, "Jesus, when He had been baptized, came up immediately from the water; and behold, the heavens were opened to Him, and He saw the Spirit of God descending like a dove and alighting upon Him. And suddenly a voice came from heaven saying, 'This is My beloved Son, in whom I am well-pleased'" (Matthew 3:16-17). This was the authenticating sealing of the divine and human Son of Man. Though Jesus knew He was the Son of God, He was given this further confirmation of the Father's seal upon His Messianic ministry.

That's very moving. The divine Son of God living in human flesh received the sealing that eventually would be administered by the Holy Spirit in those who came to believe in Him as Savior and Lord after His crucifixion and resurrection. Indeed, after Christ's ascension and glorification, He did return as reigning Lord entrusted with the Father's authority to be the Baptizer of believers with the Holy Spirit. Now Christ and the Holy Spirit work in perfect oneness and harmony to reconcile us to the Father.

This background prepares us to bring together the custom of sealing letters, documents, and objects signifying ownership and authentification, and the spiritual sealing of the Holy Spirit that consistently confirms our inheritance, convicts us of the untapped resources of our inheritance, conditions us to utilize the riches of our inheritance, and conforms us to the likeness of the One Who gave us our inheritance. All this is involved in the sealing of "the Holy Spirit of promise, Who is the guarantee of our inheritance."

⁓

The Spirit's sealing is the guarantee that
we will receive all the rest of
our inheritance.

⁓

One of my favorite paintings is "The Reading of the Will" by the Scottish artist, Sir David Wilkie. It depicts a family lawyer sitting at a table. A will is before him which he is reading through pince-nez eyeglasses on his nose. People are seated around the room leaning forward with rapt attention. An old chap has his ear-trumpet directed toward the lawyer. All are listening to the reading of the will with keen interest, waiting to hear their name and the amount of their inheritance.

Our Advocate, the Holy Spirit, Who acts as our divine lawyer, doesn't just read us the will and testament of our living Lord; rather, He is, Himself, the primary gift of the liberating legacy of our Lord. The Spirit's sealing is the guarantee that we will receive all the rest of our inheritance. The word "guarantee" in Greek means an earnest deposit, a down payment in like kind. Paul says that the sealing is a down payment "until the redemption of the purchased possession." Surely that means our continuing transformation now and at physical death, our transition to heaven. Life under the counseling of the greatest Counselor in this world is a foretaste of heaven. Our sealing begins now and continues throughout this life. Here's how it happens.

THE SEALING CONFIRMS

The Holy Spirit enables our conversion and then confirms that it has happened. He engenders the gift of faith, so we can hear and respond to the Gospel, accepting Christ as Lord. "No one can say that Jesus is Lord except by the Holy Spirit" (1 Corinthians 12:3). He melts the wax of our souls and then presses the seal of Christ into us. The sealing confirms for us that we belong to the Lord. The seal of ownership imprints us forever.

This is when the counseling ministry of the Holy Spirit begins. He helps us *know that we are known and owned* by the Lord. His assignment is to make us sure of our salvation and to give us security in Christ.

So many nominal Christians are unsure of their salvation. Often contemporary evangelists who hold crusades find that a large proportion of their converts are church members who are uncertain about their conversion. When I lead renewal conferences, I find it necessary to go back to square zero to talk about how to begin new life in Christ. Whenever I preach a sermon on the biblical plan of salvation, I receive letters from church people all over the nation telling me that they became sure of their salvation for the first time!

I always include in the plan of salvation an explanation of the sealing confirmation of the Holy Spirit as the introductory step of His continuing ministry as our Counselor. Without this sealing, a person's verbal confession of Christ as Lord and Savior is soon invaded by uncertainty and self-doubt. The assurance and security of the sealing by the Holy Spirit are lacking. Some are victims of incomplete biblical instruction. In confirmation training or inquirers' classes in preparation for church membership, they were never told about the sealing and anointing with the power of the Holy Spirit, or told that it is either necessary or possible.

~

"Holy Spirit, I ask for and thankfully receive your sealing. Help me never forget that I belong to Christ. Constantly confirm in me the assurance of the Father's eternal love and forgiveness through the cross. Fill me now with Your power that I've learned about today."

~

A man who has been visiting my church came to see me one afternoon. "I'm not really sure I'm a Christian," he said flatly as we began our conversation. He went on, "I was confirmed as a teenager and have been involved in a church through the years. I believe in Christ, but can't say that I really know Him personally. I do my best to live a Christian life—you know, a moral life playing by the rules—but it's a tough battle. Sometimes I wonder why there's so little of the joy and peace others talk about."

It was a delight to introduce this man to the greatest Counselor in the world. I went over this verse from Ephesians 1:13-14 we've been reflecting on in this chapter. After repeating the first part, "In Him [Christ] you also trusted, after you heard the word of truth, the Gospel of your salvation," I said, "You've done this—right?" He assured me he had when he joined a church years before. I went on to the second part, "In Whom also, having believed, you were sealed with the Holy Spirit of promise...." He broke in, "So what's this sealing? I've never heard about that. In fact, the Holy Spirit has

always been a mystery to me." No wonder this man felt unsure of his salvation and was frustrated by trying to live the
Christian life on his own strength!

We talked at length about the counseling ministry of the
Holy Spirit. "The first thing your Counselor wants to help
you accept is an assurance that you belong to Christ now and
for eternity. Then in daily times alone with Him, confide with
Him whenever you feel insecure or harbor self-doubt. He
wants to help you claim your inheritance as a loved and forgiven person, and encourage you to draw on the resources of
the spiritual account Christ has given you."

At the end of our visit, we prayed together. I was moved by
the man's prayer. "Holy Spirit, I ask for and thankfully receive
your sealing. Help me never forget that I belong to Christ.
Constantly confirm in me the assurance of the Father's eternal
love and forgiveness through the cross. Fill me now with Your
power that I've learned about today."

My friend had become a counselee of the Holy Spirit. Now
months later, he continues to grow as a secure man in Christ,
but not without daily sessions with his Counselor.

It is important to underline that my friend shouldn't have
had to wait those years for the sealing confirmation of the
Holy Spirit. The sealing should have been an integral part of
the explanation of what it means to be born again.

But even when the sealing has been part of our conversion,
we need daily reconfirmation that we belong to Christ, are not
our own, and have the irrevocable seal pressed into our lives.
Our Counselor won't allow us to forget. He uses our times
alone with Him to help us when insecurity raises its ugly
head. He tenderly and firmly helps us to get to the root of
feelings of insecurity resulting from unhealed memories or some
new stirring of self-doubt or the negative criticisms of others.

For Christians, insecurity is so often caused by a brief or

prolonged return to self-reliance. One thing the self is not: ultimately reliable as a source of stability and strength. After the initial enthusiasm of becoming a Christian, it's so easy to slip back into running our own lives on our own power. We may remain certain that Christ died for us and that we are going to heaven when we die, but living between now and then becomes an arduous task when we depend only on our resources.

~

We may remain certain that Christ died for us and that we are going to heaven when we die, but living between now and then becomes an arduous task when we depend only on our resources.

~

Added to this, the challenge of living faithfully in response to the "oughts" and "shoulds" of Christian ethics and responsible discipleship inevitably leads to frustration and discouragement—if we try to do it on our own steam. When we fail and become overly critical of ourselves, our Counselor is graciously waiting to draw us away from the busyness of daily life and rebuild our security in Christ. He leads us back to the cross and fresh forgiveness, and then reminds us that we were attempting a humanly impossible thing. The Christian life was never meant to be fueled by human effort alone, but by His fire. "You have been sealed with the seal of Christ," He says firmly. "You belong to Him. That will never change. Now trust Me for supernatural power to live for and glorify Christ!"

THE SEALING CONVICTS

The Holy Spirit's sealing begins a lifelong process of transformation of our thinking, character, values, and goals. He presses the seal of Christ into our lives daily with a particular emphasis on the second part of the words on the seal we quoted earlier, "Let everyone who names the name of Christ depart from iniquity." Our Counselor convicts us of any manifestations of pride, self-centeredness, and resistance to receive and communicate love, giving us the courage to change with His help.

~

Every day we do and say things that contradict that we are a new creation in Christ. Our behavior baffles us as we look back on a day or week.

~

Our initial sealing by the Spirit enables us to claim Paul's awesome promise in 2 Corinthians 5:17, "Therefore, if anyone is in Christ, he is a new creation; old things have passed away; behold, all things have become new." This assurance is a basic tenet of our inheritance. However, it is also important to note that Paul followed this soaring rhetoric about the new creation with some strong confrontational language to the Corinthians about their unrighteous behavior. They were not claiming their inheritance, but were returning to old habits and patterns of sin.

We can empathize. Every day we do and say things that contradict that we are a new creation in Christ. Our behavior baffles us as we look back on a day or week. Believing what we do, how could we have succumbed to such fantasies, felt such anger or jealousy, compromised absolute honesty in such a slick way, hurt that person with those cutting words, refused to give forgiveness, or denied the Lord in some crucial opportunity to stand for justice? Add to the list your own brand of minor sins.

Our Advocate the Holy Spirit helps convict us of these sins. He knows it's perilous for us to carry them. In our daily counseling sessions with Him, He urges us to confess each one and receive forgiveness.

But that's only the beginning. When we have shared with Him the surface sins on our minds, He begins to probe to reveal to us deeper things we've hidden behind the veil of self-righteousness. He knows the untouched flaws in our character, the uncorrected distortions in our thinking, and the unprioritized confusion of our values. He also discerns our subtle treason when we do the right thing for the wrong reason, or the wrong thing for what we've convinced ourselves is the right reason.

∼

One of the most important things that has
changed since I trusted the Holy Spirit
as my Counselor is the depth
of my confession.

∼

A woman who has become a counselee of the Holy Spirit said, "One of the most important things that has changed since I trusted the Holy Spirit as my Counselor is the depth of my confession. I used to rattle off all my little failures and mistakes when I prayed. Now, in addition, I simply ask the Holy Spirit to bring to my attention the deeper motives of what I do and say. He leads me through an inventory of my relationships and takes me back over the previous day's actions and reactions. I've had to become absolutely honest with myself and with Him. He's shown me I'm not always right (hard to admit!), helps me see things through other people's eyes, and helps me to admit that my willfulness really cripples my relationships. On the other hand, when I might be tempted to vascillate on social issues, He helps me to be sure my convictions are rooted in the Gospel and assists me to express them with His fruit of love, patience, and gentleness. And oh... I mustn't forget—also self-control. For me that fruit of the Spirit is really knowing myself and letting Him take control."

~

My constant prayer is that the Holy Spirit
would give me the gift to see myself as
He sees me.

~

The Scot Robert Burns prayed, "Oh wad some power the gift to gie us, to see ourselves as others see us!" My constant prayer is that the Holy Spirit would give me the gift to see myself as He sees me. And so I pray with Charles Wesley, "Show me, as my soul can bear, the depth of inbred sin." And He does. He helps us to be absolutely honest with ourselves.

Our Counselor leads us in a two-fold confession. The word "confess" in Greek is *homologeō*: a compound of *homos,* same; and *logo,* to speak. Confession is to agree with and say what has been spoken as a charge against us, or to repeat an assurance about which we have been reminded. The Holy Spirit enables us to articulate both. He helps us identify what we have done because of willful pride. Then He assists us to put into words our admission of sins and our longing to receive forgiveness. Next He helps us confess—accept, affirm, and experience anew—the stupendous assurance that we are forgiven. On a daily basis we receive cleansing of guilt over our failures and a chance to begin again.

The Holy Spirit never shows us our problems without also giving us a refocused vision of our potential. This leads us to the next aspect of the sealing of the Spirit.

THE SEALING THAT CONFORMS

The sealing of the Holy Spirit performs the greatest miracle offered to us in our inheritance. When God first thought of you and me, He had in mind our conformation into the image of His Son. Paul caught the glorious vision, "For whom He foreknew, He also predestined to be *conformed* to the image of his Son..." (Romans 8:29, emphasis mine).

A young lad in a confirmation class had misheard the title of the classes he had taken. He announced to his parents that on the next Sunday he was going to be "conformed." The parents were quick to correct his pronunciation, but was he so wrong? I think he was right on target. Any confirmation that isn't a vital step in conformation to the image of Christ may miss the mark.

The Holy Spirit presses the seal into our being to make us more and more like the One Who owns us. The Spirit infuses our thinking brain with the image of Christ so that all our faculties are marshalled to work cooperatively in tandem, following His inspiration of the miracle of Christlikeness He is seeking to produce in us.

We are all trying to conform to some image of what we long to become. Our image may be focused on some significant person in our lives, past or present, whom we would like to emulate. The sealing of the Holy Spirit sublimely elevates our thinking, hoping, imagining, and willing desire to Christ.

And our part? Paul was clear about that: "I beseech you therefore, brethren, by the mercies of God, that you present your bodies [your total life] a living sacrifice, holy, acceptable to God, which is your reasonable service. And do not be conformed to this world, but be transformed by the renewing of your mind, that you may prove what is that good and acceptable and perfect will of God" (Romans 12:1-2, Phillips translation, brackets added). It is important to note that both admonitions, "Do not be conformed to this world" and "Be transformed by the renewing of your mind," are in the present passive (done to us) imperative in the Greek, indicating what we should not allow to be done to us and something we should allow to be done. J.B. Phillips expresses this in his paraphrase translation, "Don't let the world around you squeeze you into its own mold, but let God remold your minds from within, so that you may prove in practice that the plan of God for you is good, meets all His demands, and moves toward the goal of true maturity."

$\sim$

The Holy Spirit presses the seal into our being to make us more and more like the One Who owns us.

$\sim$

There's never any question about this goal of true maturity—not since timeless eternity before creation. You and I have a majestic destiny that is to be our magnificent obsession: to be conformed to the image of Christ! The sealing of the Holy Spirit is for no less a purpose. It's His seal that gives us zeal to make that purpose our passion in life.

THE INNER VOICE

We are given ears to listen to the "Inner Voice" of the Holy Spirit through the sealing we have received. The lines of communication are opened so that we can listen attentively to what He has to say. This term "inner voice" was used frequently by one of my heroes in the faith. The account of how he was sealed with the Holy Spirit is true. It's recorded in his own writings and in biographical studies of his life. Family and friends attest to its validity. The last time I saw this man was in the airport in Bethlehem, Pennsylvania, after he had spoken at a retreat in my church when I was a pastor there. Just before he boarded the airplane he turned and waved good-bye raising three fingers of his right hand, a customary gesture he uses to signify, "Christ is Lord." The source of the confidence of this man was in Christ and the guidance of the "inner voice" of the Holy Spirit. It all started years before when he discovered the basic secret of yielding all that he knew of himself to receive all that God was ready to give him.

OUR ALL FOR HIS ALL

I'm talking about the outstanding missionary statesman, the late E. Stanley Jones. My personal acquaintance with him took place near the end of his life. He had rich experiences to share. As he looked back over his years of adventures in missions, he still cherished the memory of his conversion to Christ and being filled with the Holy Spirit. He was profoundly changed by his conversion in some evangelistic meetings that were held in his church. He knew Christ was his Lord and felt loved and forgiven. He said, "I was reconciled. As I arose from my knees, I felt I wanted to put my arms around the world and share this with everybody. Little did I dream at that moment that I would spend the rest of my life literally trying to put my arms around the world to share with everybody. But I have. This was a seed moment. The whole of my future was packed into it."[1]

The Holy Spirit who motivated and monitored Stanley's conversion also led him into an experience of deeper consecration and empowering. He described it as a filling of the Holy

Spirit. It was the beginning of a long and glorious succession of daily experiences of being filled.

∿

I was reconciled. As I arose from my knees, I felt I wanted to put my arms around the world and share this with everybody.

∿

A year after Stanley's conversion, he was alone in his room reading the Bible, particularly focused on the Holy Spirit in the Scriptures. He closed his Bible and dropped to his knees beside his bed, saying, "Now, Lord, what shall I do?" The Lord replied, "Will you give Me your all?" After a time of reflection Stanley replied, "Yes, Lord, of course I will. I will give you my all, all I know and all I do not know." The Lord's response was, "Then take my all, take the Holy Spirit."[2]

Stanley describes in his autobiography what happened. "I paused for a moment: my all for His All; my all was myself, His All was Himself, the Holy Spirit. I saw in a flash the offer. I eagerly replied: 'I will take the Holy Spirit!' I arose from my knees, with no evidence, save His word. I walked out on the naked promise of that word. His character was behind that word. I could trust Him to give me His all. I walked around the room repeating my acceptance. The doubts began to close in on me.... I walked around the room pushing away with my hands the menacing doubts when suddenly I was filled with the Holy Spirit. Wave after wave of the Spirit seemed to be going through me as a cleansing fire. I could only walk the floor with the tears of joy flowing down my cheeks. I could do nothing but praise Him—and did. I knew this was no passing emotion; the Holy Spirit had come to abide with me forever."[3]

And abide he did. Throughout his life Stanley had a strong mystical awareness of what he called "the Inner Voice." He depended on that voice in every crisis. "It has always been right. It has never let me down."

Perhaps the reason that Dr. Stanley Jones' life-story is so helpful is that it includes not only times of exhilaration but also of discouragement. He was as honest about these as he was about his first infilling of the Spirit. And each time he hit one of those difficult periods through overwork, the "Inner Voice" gave him the prescription for his perplexity: he needed to keep on being filled. Deeper trust, greater dependence, complete receptivity was needed.

My own experience with the "Inner Voice" of the Holy Spirit has proven to be equally reliable. He speaks through inspiration I know comes from Him. He uses a powerful blend of thought, emotion, and a mysterious inner working in our hearts to help us to know that something is right or less than best for us or the people around us. I call it the inner nudge. More specifically, the Holy Spirit raises questions, alerts me to times when I've missed the mark, and gives me the power to be different.

When I submit to the guidance of the Holy Spirit's "Inner Voice," I'm not only guided in big decisions but directed in the specifics that result in the serendipities of the Spirit-led life.

In the next chapter, we will shift our metaphors from the ministry of the Holy Spirit as sealer to potter. We are going to discover how the Spirit shapes us in Christ's image.

3 ⟩ Our Counselor's Program— God's Will in Our Lives

Recently I was driving along a lonely road through the rocky terrain of the island of Lewis, one of the western isles of Scotland. My eye spied a sign along the main road pointing to a cottage some distance off in the hills. It said, "A Potter: You Are Welcome."

I parked my car beside the road and followed a path to the solitary cottage. I've always had a special fascination for potters and their craft. It's very interesting to watch them sitting at their spinning potting wheel. Their hands are so skillful as they mold the clay into a thing of beauty. A soft piece of clay can become a magnificent vase, bowl, or pitcher.

However, this potter's work was not very impressive. The finished pieces displayed for sale did not motivate me to make a purchase. When I watched him work, I noticed his hands were clumsy. "I'm just a novice, starting to learn this craft," he explained. He didn't have to tell me; it was obvious.

Before I left the potter said, "Let me show you something." He left his potter's wheel and led me out to a shed behind the cottage. He opened the door. I was amazed at what I saw. There was a pile of literally thousands of shattered vases. "These are my failures," he said. "I just throw them in here."

"Why do you keep them?" I asked.

"They are a reminder that I'm still learning. Some day I'll be a really good potter," he responded flatly.

"Thanks for the message!" I said and started back to my car. When I looked back over my shoulder and waved good-bye, he was scratching his head with a quizzical look on his face, wondering what message he'd given his visitor.

As I drove on, I thought a lot about the parable I'd just observed. I couldn't get off my mind that shed filled with cast-off broken failures. That led me to think about a Potter who doesn't have a cast-off shed, One who keeps the clay on the wheel until it is shaped into the unique original He wants to create.

I thought of Jeremiah's experience at a potter's house (Jeremiah 18). The Lord reminded this prophet that He was the eternal Potter of his people. I also reflected on Paul's words to the Ephesians, "We are His workmanship, created in Christ Jesus for good works" (Ephesians 2:10). The Greek word for "workmanship," *poiēma*, a thing of beauty, came to mind.

Then Robert Browning's lines about the divine Artificer came to mind:

> So take and use thy work
> Amend what flaws may lurk,
> What strain o' the stuff, what warpings past the aim!
> My times are in thy hand!
> Perfect the cup as planned![1]

OUR POTTER'S HAND

Our Potter's hand is the Holy Spirit. Our lives, as well as our times, are in His hands. We are His assignment. As the clay is in a human potter's hand, so we are being molded by His hand. When we are converted, we are placed on the wheel) to be shaped into the image of what we were meant to be. We become a new creation when we are born again, but the molding of that new creation into the Potter's pattern, Christ, takes His skillful hands. He presses His loving, strong hand and skillful fingers upon us. In all of life's circumstances, the ups and downs of life, the joy and the pain, He fashions us into the people we were destined to be. It's part of our "rebirth right" and He is faithful to see it through to completion. We are not what we used to be before conversion, and, praise the Holy Spirit, we are not going to stay what we are at any stage of growth.

~

Our waiting times, when we are yielded and still to the Potter's touch, are in our daily counseling sessions with the Holy Spirit.

~

The secret of growth is submission to the Potter's hand. Years ago, Adelaide Pollard (1862-1934) experienced what she called "great distress of soul" because her plans to go to Africa as a missionary were thwarted by lack of funds. One night at a prayer meeting she realized her need to submit her will and plans to the Lord. Complete submission resulted in a profound peace. After the meeting, she penned a poem that has become a favorite hymn. It gives us words to pray and sing as the Potter's wheel begins to turn at ever increasing speed, and the Spirit's hand is placed upon us as He persists in His work.

Have Thine own way, Lord, have Thine own way,
Thou art the Potter, I am the clay.
Mold me and make me after Thy will
While I am waiting, yielded and still.[2]

Our waiting times, when we are yielded and still to the Potter's touch, are in our daily counseling sessions with the Holy Spirit. We come to Him with our greatest need and our most urgent question. We long to know the will of God for our lives, so we ask our Counselor, "How can I know God's will? How can I be sure I'm in the will of God? How do the decisions I must make today fit into Your greater will?"

THE BIG QUESTION

When I was preparing to write this book, I asked my congregation and my radio and television audiences to respond to the question, "If you had a prolonged time with the Holy Spirit, the greatest Counselor in the world, what would you want to talk about?" The largest category of the thousands of responses was about guidance in the will of God.

∾

"Holy Spirit, what are You making? What is the plan You are following in shaping my life? How does this decision I'm facing relate to this curvature Your fingers are impressing in my character?"

∾

I was not surprised. I've been doing yearly surveys of people's needs for twenty-five years in preparation for planning my sermons. Every year a large percentage of the responses are about how to be sure of the will of God and how to receive daily guidance. Why is this? Perhaps it's because many have not discovered how the Holy Spirit functions as the communicator and interpreter of God's ultimate will, plus giving us daily guidance for our lives. Thus when life becomes difficult or uncertain, we need reassurance that the cup of our lives is being shaped as planned.

There's a question asked in Isaiah 45:9 that we want to ask, "Shall the clay say to him who forms it, 'What are You making?'" Originally, that was a presumptuous question of a resistant, apostate Israel to whom Isaiah prophesied. But now in the post-Pentecost age of the Holy Spirit, we can ask the same question with a very different tone. "Holy Spirit, what are You making? What is the plan You are following in shaping my life? How does this decision I'm facing relate to this curvature Your fingers are impressing in my character?"

THE AWESOME ANSWER

The answer we are given is in ten words the Holy Spirit inspired the apostle Paul to write to the Thessalonians. It is very moving when, in the counseling sessions with the Holy Spirit we call prayer, He brings to mind verses of Scripture which He inspired. When He breathes life into them, they leap off the pages of the Bible. These nine words from 1 Thessalonians 4:3 have that impelling, lively quality now. "For this is the will of God, your sanctification."

At first, this seems like a ponderous answer to our feverish urgency to know God's will for some urgent decision we're facing today. Usually, the only time we think about God's will is when there is some hard choice to make. So we rush into prayer blurting, "Holy Spirit, hurry up. What am I to do?" Often the Spirit graciously gives us an answer for a pressing need, but He longs for us to spend consistent daily times with

Him in prayer, so we can catch the big picture of the divine plan for our lives.

~

Preparation for receiving answers to specific guidance in the will of God comes out of an experience and knowledge of the sublime will of God. And that sublime will is that we be sanctified.

~

Over the years, I have discovered a liberating secret. I must relearn it often. When I do, it puts everything into perspective. Here's the discovery from thousands of counseling sessions with the greatest Counselor in the world: preparation for receiving answers to specific guidance in the will of God comes out of an experience and knowledge of the sublime will of God. And that sublime will is that we be sanctified.

MORE THAN A THEOLOGICAL TERM

Sanctification is more than an esoteric word for highly trained theologians to banter about. It's a magnificent word that describes the Potter's pattern, the image He follows in producing the "workmanship," the person He wants to help you and me become.

When we take the Greek word for sanctification apart, we realize that it's rooted in the word "holy." Sanctification is the process of being made holy. What does that have to do with the will of God, or more precisely with the choices we must make today? Everything! The assignment of the Holy Spirit is to counsel us in becoming what we are already. That's not meant to be clever rhetoric.

Here's the point. "Holy" means set apart, belonging to God. Long before we became Christians God predestined us to belong to him. His choice came long before we chose to receive Christ as our Lord and Savior. He called us before we called out to Him for His help, love, and forgiveness. I didn't just dream up this order of things. Christ made it very clear, "You did not choose me but I chose you" (John 15:16). And He left no doubt that it was by the Father's prior election that people came to Him and chose to follow Him. "All that the Father gives Me will come to Me, and the one who comes to Me I will by no means cast out" (John 6:37). All three persons of the Trinity are active in our conversion. The Father elects; Christ attracts; the Holy Spirit contacts.

◠

All three persons of the Trinity are active in our conversion. The Father elects; Christ attracts; the Holy Spirit contacts.

◠

The Bible's special word to designate those who belong to God through His choice and Christ's voice is itself rooted in the word "holy." We are the saints, the holy ones. We belong first and foremost to God. So the clay of our lives that is placed on the divine wheel for the Holy Spirit to mold already belongs to God, but it needs daily shaping into all that God wants for those who belong to Him. And the Potter knows what He is doing. Notice His first name, "Holy." The Holy Spirit is God's Spirit.

THE BEST OF ALL COUNSELORS

Any effective human counselor must have a clear understanding of wholeness in order to be able to discern the needs of a person who has asked for help. His or her training is not only in the disorders and proclivities of human nature, but also in what a healthy integrated person is like. This image of wholeness becomes the motivating factor in listening, caring, and probing. His or her task is to discern the roadblocks keeping a counselee from living a full, rewarding, happy life. The challenge is to help the counselee to see these impediments and change behavior patterns that cause them. We are thankful for those who have this crucial calling.

~

Anytime we come to our Counselor for advice on our decisions and want to know God's will, He sees every step we are to take in the perspective of our sanctification.

~

The vision of wholeness of the greatest Counselor in the world is one in which He was intimately involved, both before time and in history. His pattern, as He works with us as our Potter, is Jesus Christ. As we said in the first chapter, Jesus Christ in His incarnate life not only revealed God as He is but what we are meant to be. The divine and human were perfectly blended. We were meant to love, forgive, heal, and live as he lived. That's the wondrous secret of the Christian life. Paul longed for Christ to be formed in the Galatians (Galatians 4:19). He declared the awesome potential to the Colossians, "Christ in you, the hope of glory" (Colossians 1:27).

The ministry of the Holy Spirit is to glorify Christ in us and to enable us to grow in His likeness. Sanctification is sublimely that: growth in the likeness of Christ. Therefore, these magnificent nine words spell out the Spirit's role perfectly: "For this is the will of God, your sanctification." The goal of all this is clearly stated by a further Spirit-inspired word to the Thessalonians, "Now may the God of peace Himself sanctify you completely; and may your whole spirit, soul, and body be preserved blameless at the coming of our Lord Jesus Christ. He

Who calls you is faithful, Who also will do it" (1 Thessalonians 5:23-24).

Anytime we come to our Counselor for advice on our decisions and want to know God's will, He sees every step we are to take in the perspective of our sanctification. Will it move us forward in being made holy, more completely like Christ, in spirit, soul, and body?

THE SUBSTANTIVE ELEMENTS OF
OUR SANCTIFICATION

Let's briefly take a look at these substantive elements of our human nature. It will help us immeasurably in discovering the will of God.

First, the Holy Spirit wants to sanctify our spirits. Where is our spirit in us? Our first response is to say that the spirit of a person is in his or her emotions. I'm more inclined to suggest that our spirit is in our minds. Paul spoke of the spirit of our minds: "Be renewed in the spirit of your mind" (Ephesians 4:23). The spirit of the mind is the port of entry for the Spirit of God. He wants to capture and seeks to pervade the cerebral cortex, the thinking brain. The brain is the control center for our perception, memory, imagination, and volition as well as our emotions and the functioning of our nervous system and the totality of our physiology. Jesus said, "God is Spirit, and those who worship Him must worship in spirit and truth" (John 4:24). He also added mind to the ancient Hebrew Shema, "You shall love the Lord your God with all your heart, with all your soul, with *all your mind,* and with all your strength" (Mark 12:30, emphasis mine).

I'll probably not get very far by suggesting that we change the chorus "Into my heart" to "Into my mind." It may be dif-

ficult to imagine a congregation giving up the attachment to
the old words and singing, "Into my mind, into my brain,
come into my mind, Lord Jesus; come in today, come in to
stay...." Yet that's what we need to pray. The Holy Spirit
wants to give us minds that are focused on Christ and the grand
purpose of glorifying Him in all that we do and say.

Further, the thinking brain is the control center for discerning and doing the will of God. We have to think through
issues under the guidance of the Holy Spirit. Once He helps
us arrive at what's best, it is the brain that triggers the will to
act on the guidance we've received. The emotional impetus to
follow through is also instigated by the thinking brain. What's
in our feelings has first been in our brains!

~

*The Holy Spirit wants to give us minds that are focused
on Christ and the grand purpose of glorifying Him
in all that we do and say.*

~

The next substantive element involved in the sanctification
that is God's will for us is our souls. Paul used the word *psyche*
in Greek for this element. It represented the immaterial, invisible part of a person, his or her essential life, or more precisely,
his or her own *self*. I like to think of the influence of the soul
in terms of our character and personality.

Our character is made up of the values and patterns that
determine our behavior: our personality, the manner and disposition of our distinctive self. Both character and personality
are crucial in the Holy Spirit's sanctifying process. He wants
to mold our character, our moral and behavioral values, around
Christ. The result is that our personalities become a unique
manifestation of Christlyness. The Holy Spirit is wonderfully
original in producing each of us in distinctly different ways.
We don't have to be like we've been, or a cookie-cutter stamp

of some other person. Instead, each of us is called to be a manifestation of Christlyness showing forth Christ's character traits enumerated in the fruit of the Spirit: love, joy, peace, patience, kindness, goodness, faithfulness, gentleness, and self-control (Galatians 5:22-23).

~

The Holy Spirit is wonderfully original in producing each of us in distinctly different ways. We don't have to be like we've been, or a cookie-cutter stamp of some other person.

~

The third substantive element the Holy Spirit seeks to sanctify, as part of the full realization of the will of God for us, is our bodies. Along with our minds and souls, our bodies are sacred and holy, belonging to the Lord. Looking into a mirror, particularly a full-length one, you may exclaim, "So what's so holy about that?" Yet what we see in the mirror is a temple. Paul asks, "Do you not know that your body is the temple of the Holy Spirit who is in you, whom you have from God, and you are not your own? For you were bought at a price; therefore glorify God in your body and in your spirit, which are God's" (1 Corinthians 6:19-20).

Thinking of our bodies as temples of the Holy Spirit puts the care of them into a whole different perspective. It changes our attitude toward how we eat, exercise, rest, and keep fit physically. It also gives us a guide for our sexuality. Nonmarital, extramarital, and perverted sexual expressions are desecrations of the temple of the Holy Spirit. So are overeating, drinking too much, or addictive habits.

SPECIFIC GUIDANCE

Once we understand that God's sublime will for all of us is our sanctification, we are able to receive specific guidance in our daily decisions. Our counseling sessions with the Holy Spirit are to be done in that context. His greatest concern is to help us remember that we belong to God and are programmed for greatness—to be made like Christ. With this in mind we spread out before the Holy Spirit the choices and decisions before us. In response He leads us through some very crucial steps.

∾

"Let go, give over your anxiety, give up your imperious will. There will be an answer when you are free to receive."

∾

The first step is thanksgiving. The Holy Spirit gave Paul that secret long ago. "In everything give thanks; for this is the will of God in Christ Jesus for you" (1 Thessalonians 5:18). Everything? Yes! The Holy Spirit brings us to the place where we can give thanks, actually praise to God, for the choices and decisions that face us—big and small, difficult and challenging, complex and painful. He knows that praise is the ultimate relinquishment, the final release of our tight grip of control. Only through praising God for the problem do we acknowledge that nothing happens without His permission and everything surrendered to Him will be used for our growth and His glory.

This quality of praise and thanksgiving is not our natural inclination. We're used to counting our blessings after they happen. Prospective thanksgiving is a supernatural gift from the Holy Spirit. He enables us to give thanks for the uncertainty about our choices and decisions as well as the challenges or problems that have caused them. He counsels us, "Let go, give over your anxiety, give up your imperious will. There will be an answer when you are free to receive."

The second step is confession. The Holy Spirit knows that we cannot receive the guidance we need if we are carrying any baggage of unconfessed sin, unforgiven hurts in our relationships, or anger and hostility toward any other person. Confession under His leadership also includes honest admission of times we have been disobedient in following His previous guidance. There's a great difference between knowledge of the will of God and general intellectual knowledge of truth. The secret of receiving guidance is obedience. The Holy Spirit puts us through the paces until He is sure we are serious about doing what He will reveal to us.

The third step is probing questions. The Holy Spirit penetrates with urgent questions to help us get to what is best. In the quiet of counseling prayer He asks,

1. What choice will glorify God in every way?

2. Will the decision enable your growth in Christlikeness in your mind, soul, and body?

3. Is the decision in keeping with the Ten Commandments, Jesus' commandment to love others as He has loved us, and His admonition to seek first God's kingdom and righteousness?

4. Will the decision bring the *"ultimate"* good of all concerned? The word ultimate is used because some choices we must make bring temporary hardship, but lead us and the people involved on to greater growth and maturity.

5. Will the decision jeopardize your ability to tithe? No choice is right that makes us embezzlers of the first tenth of all of our income that belongs to God for His work.

6. Can you happily invite the Lord into every aspect of the implications of the decision? Could He be a partner in accomplishing the cause, venture, or relationship?

7. What are the real motives behind a particular choice?

These are the questions the Holy Spirit has asked me through the years. Through consistent counseling with Him, giving ourselves time for a decision to be nurtured by Him, we begin to trust Him *and* ourselves a lot more. If the dominant desire of our hearts is to know and do God's will, His Spirit can convert what I call our "wanter." When our desires are saturated by the Holy Spirit and our wills are completely surrendered, He creates in us a desire to do what He knows is best. Instead of thinking, "If I want to do this, surely it must be wrong," we come to trust the inner nudges of the Spirit through our purified desires.

~

When our desires are saturated by the Holy Spirit and our wills are completely surrendered, He creates in us a desire to do what He knows is best.

~

Recently, I was praying for a person to fill a key position in the pastoral leadership of my church in Hollywood. As I was praying, feeling the pressure on me because this post was vacant, suddenly a man's name and face came to mind. I kept on praying about him as I spent the following week researching his commitment, experience, and gifts. The man was perfect! The following Saturday I saw him at a meeting. Again the Inner Voice of the Holy Spirit confirmed His previous guidance, "This is the one. It is he you should call to this job."

A broad smile spread across Doug Millham's face when I told him I needed to visit with him. "I've not been able to get you off my mind," I said. I told him about the need for a person of his qualifications for the position.

"It's not surprising to hear you say that I've been on your mind," he responded. "I've had you on my mind constantly for a week." He had learned about the position that had been vacated. Even though he was the very successful leader of a Christian organization, he felt an "Inner Voice" telling him he should be open to being considered if I ever talked to him about the possibility of becoming the executive pastor of the Hollywood Presbyterian Church.

After a lot of meetings and prayer times together, Doug was called and is now in place giving dynamic leadership.

∼

I can think of a thousand times in my relationship with my wife, children, or friends when I wish I had listened to the "Inner Voice" sooner and followed the Holy Spirit's instructions with greater alacrity.

∼

Sometimes the Inner Voice of the Holy Spirit interrupts me with "on the spot" correctives. The other day I was involved in a fast-moving discussion with the pastoral staff of my church. In response to a suggestion made by a young pastor, I made an unnecessarily sharp retort that cut him off at the knees. He looked shocked, and I looked like an inept leader.

The fast-flowing discussion moved on. After a few minutes, the "Inner Voice" said, "Stop the discussion and apologize to your brother!" If the years have taught me anything, I've learned to obey orders from the "Inner Voice" of the Holy Spirit. So I said, "Before this discussion goes any further, I want to reel it back to something I said for which I need to apologize. I turned to the young pastor, "Please forgive me. My retort a few moments ago was uncalled for and abrasive. Please accept my apology."

"Apology accepted," the man said, so we moved on.

I can think of a thousand times in my relationship with my wife, children, or friends when I wish I had listened to the "Inner Voice" sooner and followed the Holy Spirit's instructions with greater alacrity.

But my memory is filled with even more times when following orders really paid off in what's ultimately important. A nudge to make a phone call and the response from a person in need, "How did you know that I was really up against it?" Or a letter the Holy Spirit guides, which is perfectly timed by Him, and then the response: "Your letter arrived on a day when I needed to know someone was praying for me more than any day of my life." Or the compelling guidance to add an illustration to a sermon, and a person comes out of church shaking his head in wonderment, "You must have tapped my phone lines! How did you know that was exactly what I needed to hear?" Or in a conversation, I feel led to open myself up and share some discovery or lesson learned in difficulty, and the other person is utterly amazed I knew what to say. The test for me is to be sure I don't take the credit but identify the real source.

Little stuff? Perhaps. But the longer I live under the counseling ministry of the Holy Spirit, the more I discover that there's nothing too insignificant for His omniscience or His specific guidance. And we all know how little things can grow into big things. Little mistakes, minor decisions, seemingly insignificant departures from what we know is just and honest, gracious or kind, can have monstrous implications later on.

It may surprise you that one of my favorite passages in the Book of Acts is when the Holy Spirit said, "No!" It was said by the "Inner Voice" to Paul and Timothy after the young disciple was recruited by the apostle. Perhaps Timothy's first learning experience about the guidance of the Holy Spirit was what He forbade and eventually enabled (Acts 16:6-10).

Leaving Lystra, Paul, Silas, and Timothy went through Phrygia and the region of Galatia, intending to preach the Gospel in Asia Minor. They were forbidden by the Holy Spirit to do it. So they pressed on to Mysia and tried to go into Bithynia. Again, the Spirit did not permit them. Eventually the Spirit guided them to Troas on the Aegean Sea coast. It was there the apostle was given the vision of a man of Macedonia calling him to come over to Macedonia to help them. All of the decisive "nos" led toward the Holy Spirit's great "yes!" in the call to begin the conquest of Europe with the Gospel. The doors the Holy Spirit closed led to the open door He had ready. Asia Minor came later according to His timing.

Disappointment in getting what we want when we want it, if surrendered to the Holy Spirit, can lead us to His divine appointment. Who'd want to be anywhere but in his or her designated Troas if that's the Holy Spirit's embarkment site for the Lord's next big move?

And the good news is that the times of decisions will be used by the Potter to mold us. Never forget He has no cast-off shed filled with discarded people pottery. He's the greatest Counselor in the world, and He's shaping us to live forever!

4) Strength in Our Weakness

"I'VE GOT A PROBLEM...," a man said, opening a conversation at a conference recently.

"Tell me about it," I responded with empathy.

"You're looking at him!" he confided with intensity. "I've got lots of problems, but I guess I'm the biggest one. There must be something wrong with me. I've had lots of answers to prayer, but recently I haven't known what to ask for in my prayers. Some of the problems being faced by people I love are beyond me. And many of my own problems are so complex that I can't get enough of a handle on them to even know how to pray about them. I hear Christ's promise, 'Whatever you ask in my name, I will do it.' That's fine, if I just knew what to ask!"

"I've got a problem too," I said.

"Really?" the man exclaimed with surprise.

"You're looking at him!" I said with a smile.

We both laughed. I went on to share that I really understood how he was feeling. "There are times when I face problems that resist solutions and times when my worry over people whom I love brings me to the realization that I don't know what's best to pray. Also there are times when I feel a longing for a deeper relationship with the Lord, but don't know what's wrong so I can ask Him to help me make it right. But I have made some discoveries about what to do in those times. The Holy Spirit helps us in our weakness when we don't know how or what to pray. I'd be glad to share that what I'm finding really works."

"Sure," my friend replied, "I thought I was losing my faith. But if you say you sometimes hit the same snags, I really want to hear what you've discovered."

∼

The Father is seeking to work all things together for our good, the Holy Spirit Who knows His mind for what is best is working within us to help us to know what that is and how to pray for it, and the Son is making intercession for us, bringing our prayers to the Father's heart in His own name.

∼

From the level ground of a shared need, I opened my Bible and read Romans 8:26-28: "Likewise the Spirit also helps in our weaknesses. For we do not know what we should pray for as we ought, but the Spirit Himself makes intercession for us with groanings which cannot be uttered. And He Who searches the hearts knows what the mind of the Spirit is, because He makes intercession for the saints according to the will of God. And we know that all things work together for good to those who love God, to those who are the called according to His purpose."

Here is the Trinity at work in our lives. The Father is seeking to work all things together for our good, the Holy Spirit Who knows His mind for what is best is working within us to help us to know what that is and how to pray for it, and the

Son is making intercession for us, bringing our prayers to the Father's heart in His own name.

That's really encouraging. We all face times when we find it difficult to pray. Like my friend at the conference, we don't know how or what to pray. The Holy Spirit gives us strength in those times of weakness. What I shared with this fellow struggler that day is essentially what I want to communicate in this chapter. Romans 8:26-28, which I quoted to him and explained from my own discoveries, answers four of our deepest questions: When does the Holy Spirit provide? How does He penetrate? Why does He prevail? And, what does He produce?

WHEN DOES THE SPIRIT PROVIDE?

It is precisely at the point of our struggle to know how and what to pray that the Holy Spirit is ready to help us. Paul gives us a liberating conviction to change our attitude toward these times. "The Spirit helps us in our weaknesses." Now, that's really good news! The Holy Spirit takes up His most powerful work at the very time we may be tempted to give up. There's an advantage in what we thought was a disadvantage; there's hopefulness in the very recognition of our helplessness. The Spirit "helps us in our present limitations" is the way J.B. Phillips translates Paul's assurance. The New English Bible renders it, "The Spirit comes to the aid of our weaknesses." Our Counselor helps us when we find it difficult to cope. Our sense of helplessness does not disqualify us in our prayers, but actually prepares us to pray honestly.

The late Dr. Ole Hallesby, one of Norway's leading preachers and teachers, in his classic, *Prayer*, wrote, "Helplessness is unquestionably the first and surest indication of a praying heart. As far as I can see, prayer has been ordained only for the helpless. It is the last resort of the helpless; indeed, the very last way out. We try everything before we finally resort to prayer. This is not only true of us before our conversion. Prayer is our last resort throughout our whole Christian life. I know very well that we offer many and beautiful prayers, both privately and publicly, without helplessness as the impelling power. But I am not at all positive that this is prayer. Prayer and helplessness are inseparable. Only he who is helpless can truly pray."[1]

Some may think that's an overstatement, but it does open the door to prayer at our most difficult times of struggle. Far from being excluded from prayer, our times of struggle, when we feel our weakness, can be the very time when we are opened up to receive what the Holy Spirit has had ready to give us.

◆

In a time of weakness, the best way to help ourselves is to be receptive to the help of the Holy Spirit.

◆

When Paul talks about our weaknesses in Romans 8:26, he pictures a state of near collapse. Strength is draining out. As our backs feel the strain under a load of care, we say with Thomas Fuller, "Lord, strengthen my back or lighten my load." Our hearts quiver with worry and fear. Without help, defeat is sure. At this stage of our abject state of struggle, the Holy Spirit begins His strengthening in our weakness. Our extremity becomes His opportunity.

I've tried to stress this discovery, because listening to people over the years and staying in touch with what sometimes happens in my own spiritual life, I have found that at times of weakness we become our own worst enemies. Instead of accepting the extremity as the Holy Spirit's opportunity, we condemn ourselves. The "if onlys" attack with force. "If only I loved God more, I wouldn't be in this struggle." "If only I had prayed more or read the Bible more consistently, I would not be in this state of weakness." "There must be some hidden sin in my life that has caused this!'"

All of the above may be true, but they are evasions. We still think we can do something to help ourselves. In a time of weakness, the best way to help ourselves is to be receptive to the help of the Holy Spirit. So you're weak. Who isn't at times? Be thankful that these are the very times when we can be helped!

HOW DOES THE SPIRIT PENETRATE?

We are ready for our second question. How does the Spirit help us in our struggles? How does He penetrate to the core issues in our lives? He begins with our feeble explanation of what we think is our problem, or a problem in someone else we love, or some perplexity life has dished out to us. We agree with Paul's analysis of us at this point of our weakness, "For we do not know what we should pray for as we ought, *but...* [the conjunction has great force] the Spirit Himself makes intercession for us with groanings which cannot be uttered" (Romans 8:26, emphasis mine). In the original Greek manuscripts the words "for us" are omitted.

This has led some biblical interpreters to suggest that it is we who do the groaning and not the Holy Spirit. D.M. Lloyd-Jones makes a strong case for this idea. "The Holy Spirit is one of the three Persons of the Holy Trinity. He never groans; He never sighs; that is inconceivable. The Godhead does not groan.... There is no lack of knowledge in the Holy Spirit. He knows all things... and there is no cause for groaning. The groaning is in ourselves. It is we who do the groaning in a wordless manner; it is we who fail to find words to express what is happening in us."[2]

Though the rest of Dr. Lloyd-Jones' exposition of this verse is extremely helpful, I think he may have overstated his case that the Holy Spirit does not groan within us or bring us to the place of groaning over our dilemmas. The reflexive pronoun "Himself" stresses this. "The Spirit *Himself* makes intercession with groanings which cannot be uttered."

The Greek word for "groan" is *stenagmoĭs*, and like the verb *stenazō* it denotes deep sighing filled with grief and sorrow, distress and anguish.

So who does the groaning? The Spirit or us? I think both. The Holy Spirit broods over, around, and in us in our times of need. He really experiences grief over what we are enduring (Ephesians 4:30). He doesn't just groan in aloof sympathy but with real empathy over what's happening to us, with yearning not just that we get to the core of the problem, but that He gets to the core of us. I think He groans over the residuals of pride in us that resist relinquishment to the Father's will.

∽

The Holy Spirit broods over, around, and in us in our times of need. He really experiences grief over what we are enduring.

∽

There are five words the Holy Spirit wants us to come to believe: *God Himself is the answer.* Whatever else we get out of our weaknesses, unless they bring us to deeper intimacy with the Father, they will have been wasted. The Holy Spirit is constantly working to help us get the most out of suffering or difficulties. He penetrates deep within us until He reaches the logjam in us blocking the flow of willingness to trust in God more completely.

We also groan. In the midst of outward difficulties in our lives or relationships, we feel a profound sigh, a longing, a yearning. It is too deep for words. We feel an incompleteness in ourselves.

At the same time, we become acutely aware of the pain and

suffering around us. We have been called out of a fallen creation filled with pain and agony over sickness and death, misunderstandings and broken relationships. Then as the Holy Spirit draws us closer to our destiny as sons and daughters of the Father, we realize how short a distance we've come in our sanctification, being made like Christ. Previously in Romans 8, Paul described this groaning. It's actually a sign of the Holy Spirit at work in us. "And not only they, but ourselves also who have the firstfruits of the Spirit, even we ourselves groan within ourselves, eagerly waiting for the adoption, the redemption of our body" (v. 23).

Our real problem is to let go and grow. As for others around us and society, we anguish over what still remains untouched, unchanged.

Then it dawns on us. Our real problem is to let go and grow. As for others around us and society, we anguish over what still remains untouched, unchanged. We realize that we have been given the privilege of feeling the pulse of the heart of God's love for us, others, and our world. It's at this level of awareness and raw-nerve sensitivity to reality that the Holy Spirit reaches us at the deepest depths of our being to lift us to pray in the highest levels of His power.

WHY THE SPIRIT PREVAILS

This is why the Holy Spirit prevails. He prevails until we are ready to pray. He wants to help us pray at two levels. The first is in the prayers He helps us articulate. Let's be very personal and practical about how this happens. At this very moment I'm writing this, like you, I have people for whom I'm deeply concerned—loved ones, friends, people at work, many others on a long prayer list who have asked me to pray for them. There are still others on my heart who, as yet, have not admitted their need for prayer. Also, like you, I'm facing challenges for which, on my own, I simply don't know what's best. Added to this, again like you, I have opportunities to serve in which I long to know the Lord's maximum plan. Topping all this, is the yearning we share to stay on the growing edge of becoming the persons we were meant to be.

There is something else I suspect we have in common. In our prayers we often recite our long shopping list of concerns and needs and then conclude our prayer time by saying, "Well, Lord, You know what's best and so I leave all this in Your care!" We do all the talking and end the monologue without waiting for a reply. That's a cop-out and it's not real prayer.

Recently a man came to see me. "I've come to ask your advice about a difficulty I'm facing," he said. Then he began what became a forty-five minute, nonstop recitation of what was wrong. When he finally took a breath and I was about to respond, he said, "Well, thanks for listening!" and left. I stood there with my mouth hanging open and my heart filled with lots of care I wish I could have shared.

Sure, that's an extreme example of a person who loved the sound of his own voice and didn't really want any advice, but the experience reminded me of how I used to treat the Holy Spirit in what I had called prayer.

Years ago, when I first became a counselee of the Holy Spirit, He taught me how to use my time with Him much more creatively. He revealed to me that after praise, confession, and thanksgiving, I should briefly spread out before Him the needs and concerns that were on my mind and heart. Also, I learned to ask Him to bring to the surface other issues that needed to be exposed.

Then I discovered that before I actually prayed for others,

myself, and specific situations, I needed to be quiet and listen. That was not easy at first, but as I tried it I was amazed at how shallow my prayers had been. In the quiet, the Holy Spirit actually led me into a deeper understanding of people and circumstances. When I asked what and how to pray, I was given wisdom and discernment beyond my human abilities or analysis. Petitions were actually worded for me. Sensing that they came from the Lord through the Holy Spirit, you can be sure that I articulated them with boldness and assurance.

~

Then I discovered that before I actually prayed for others, myself, and specific situations, I needed to be quiet and listen.

~

You see, the Holy Spirit is no nondirective counselor who simply listens without a response, supposing that if we talk long enough we'll come to the right conclusion. He works through our minds to help us think what is the Lord's best for us and others, so we can pray inspired petitions. We were created for communion with the Lord, and the Holy Spirit enables the conversation in which we don't just relinquish our needs but in which intercessions and supplications are actually guided by Him.

All this is backed up by a very important passage of Scripture that's a vital corollary promise to the one we're considering in Romans 8:26. It's 1 Corinthians 2:9-16. Here's an explanation of how the Holy Spirit works to reveal how and what we should pray:

"Eye has not seen, nor ear heard, nor have entered into the heart of man the things which God has prepared for those who love Him." But God has revealed them to us through His Spirit. For the Spirit searches all things, yes, the deep things of God. For what man knows the things of a man except the spirit of the man which is in him? Even so no one knows the things of God except the Spirit of God. Now we have received, not the spirit of the world, but the Spirit who is from God, that we might know the things that have been freely given to us by God. These things we also speak, not in words which man's wisdom teaches but which the Holy Spirit teaches, comparing spiritual things with spiritual. But the natural man does not receive the things of the Spirit of God, for they are foolishness to him; nor can he know them, because they are spiritually discerned. But he who is spiritual judges all things, yet he himself is rightly judged by no one. For "Who has known the mind of the Lord that he may instruct Him?" But we have the mind of Christ.

I've experienced this repeatedly. My outward struggle with a problem, concern for a person, or worry over a situation has drawn me into deeper counseling sessions with my Counselor. After pressing me to the point of relinquishment of the problem and showing me that my real struggle has been to trust, then He actually reveals how I should pray, what I dare ask for, what I should have the audacity to claim.

But there's an even greater assurance here. The Holy Spirit takes our mumbling, disjointed, mixed-up words, so often jumbled in with our own selfish desires, and edits the whole thing! He cleans up our prayers, deletes, adds to, and makes sense of them. His role as our Advocate, *Parakletos*, is enacted sublimely. Just as a lawyer for the defense helps his client know what to say and how to say it, so too the Holy Spirit helps us so that our prayers are ready to be presented by Jesus Christ, our Advocate with the Father.

So even after the Holy Spirit has smelted and purified our desires, He still has to take any impurities from the wording of our prayers, so they can pass the test of being fully in keeping with the power and authority of the name of our Lord.

There are those times when all we can do is groan in our prayer. Who hasn't cried out, "Father, help me!" "Father, help my loved one!" "Father, take this situation. I don't know what to do!" Even then, the Holy Spirit puts our pleas into the right words to reach the heart of the Father.

～

The Holy Spirit takes our mumbling, disjointed, mixed-up words, so often jumbled in with our own selfish desires, and edits the whole thing!

～

Something more must be said. It's about what's called the prayer language of the Holy Spirit. Jude calls it praying in the Spirit (Jude 20). Rather than theorizing about this wonderful gift, allow me simply to share my own experience. Often in times of need, I receive the gift of a prayer language that bursts forth from within me. This gift of the Holy Spirit is beyond words and not in my native tongue or any other human language. It's not like English or any other language I've learned. It flows from my groaning heart. Indeed, it is the Holy Spirit's prayer through me. Most often when I am quiet after using this gift, I am given deeper insight into the mystery of God's will, or I see things that I previously had not understood.

As Paul makes clear in 1 Corinthians 14:13-15, this prayer language is not a substitute for praying with understanding, but in addition to prayers in which we understand what we are saying: "I will pray with the spirit, and I will also pray with understanding." The Holy Spirit prays through us in our native language and can also pray through us in a prayer language that releases our spirits to be receptive to what we had not been able to articulate before. The gift is not the sign of being a "super Christian." It simply attests to one additional way that our "groanings too deep for words" can be sent from our hearts to the Father through Christ by the Spirit.

WHAT DOES THE SPIRIT PROVIDE?

We are ready for our last question about how the Holy Spirit gives us strength in our weaknesses, "What does He provide?" Romans 8:28 answers that question in a magnificent way. We are provided knowledge. Out of the struggle to stay afloat in the tumultuous waves of doubt and adversity, the Spirit brings us into a safe harbor. Only He could get us through the channel, avoiding the rocks and shoals that could have scuttled us. And here's the verse that becomes the mooring in the secure harbor: "For we know that to those who love God; in all things God works together for good to those who are called according to His purpose" (my translation from the Greek).

~

It is God Who makes all things in our lives work together for good, His ultimate good.

~

You will note that translation is different from the way most English Bibles render Romans 8:28, "And we know that all things work together for good to those who love God, to those who are the called according to His purpose" (NKJV). Early Greek manuscripts of Romans have *ho Theos*, God, as the subject of *sunergei*, works together. This is Paul's thrust anyhow. It is God Who makes all things in our lives work together for good, His ultimate good. Therefore, in a difficult time of struggle, through the inspiration of the Holy Spirit, we *know*, (and the Greek word for "know" means to know with assurance) that God works things together for good, not just that things work together for good.

Do you see what's happened? The Holy Spirit has moved us away from our struggle to try to make things work out on our own. He has done a miracle in our thinking. For the moment nothing has changed, yet everything is different. We know by the Holy Spirit's confirmation that God is in charge and will arrange things to work out according to His purposes. Added to that, the Holy Spirit gives us the gift of practical working faith in addition to our primary faith in Christ as Savior and Lord. We come to a firm conviction that God is working His plans out even in our struggles. Why? Because the Holy Spirit makes us sure that we are among those "called according to His purpose."

~

So often we want things to work out for the temporary goal of success—all the money we think we need or being number one on people's hit parade.

~

When we don't know how or what to pray for, we can be sure that the Holy Spirit simply will lead us to pray, "Lord, work all that I'm going through into your ultimate purpose." So often we want things to work out for the temporary goal of success—all the money we think we need or being number one on people's hit parade. What He's concerned about is shaping us into the image of Christ. We can be confident that He will work everything into a wondrous pattern to bring about that purpose.

SECURITY IN OUR STRUGGLES

The only way to survive in life's struggles is to be sure we belong to God. Review the train of Paul's thought as inspired by the Holy Spirit in this passage in Romans 8. First, the Spirit helps those who acknowledge their need of help when they don't know how to pray in life's struggles. He helps us know what to pray and formulates the prayers we can't even put into words. Then He gives us the assurance that God is in control—that He is working things out, and not that, by some fate, things somehow work out.

Next the Holy Spirit inspired Paul to spell out the awesome truth of our election to be God's people. Look at what the Holy Spirit has to say to us through the apostle's words in Romans 8:29-30:

> For whom He foreknew, He also predestined to be conformed to the image of His Son, that He might be the first-born among many brethren. Moreover, whom He predestined, those He also called; whom He called, these He also justified; and whom He justified, these He also glorified.

Before time, God had you and me in His plans. We didn't happen on our time in history by accident. God's long-range view of the horizon of human history had you and me focused in His vision. That's what the verb "predestined" really means. In Greek it is *proorizō*, a compound word of "before" and "horizon." God marked us out, before we were born, determined before our experience of His grace that we were chosen to be called.

∼

Before time, God had you and me in His plans. We didn't happen on our time in history by accident.

∼

All that God did in sending His Son was so that we might know and love Him as our Father. Christ lived on earth, proclaimed the kingdom of God, died on the cross, and was raised up for you and me. This is the good news of the Gospel that grips us because we were chosen to believe. Through Christ, we were called because we were already chosen. Through the cross, we were loved and forgiven, reconciled and redeemed. That's what it means to be justified. We have been made right with the Father in and through the righteousness of Christ. And for us, as those who have chosen to accept our chosen-ness, the Holy Spirit has been poured out to fill us and make us like Christ. And that's what it means to be glorified!

If all those settled assurances don't give us security in our struggles, nothing will. Nevertheless, life is demanding and saps our strength. That's why the Holy Spirit never gives up in His constant efforts to remind us that, in spite of anything that happens to us or around us, we have the security of our status as elected sons and daughters of the Father and are called and chosen as disciples of His Son. The Holy Spirit persistently is the Spirit of adoption "by Whom we cry out, 'Abba, Father'" (Romans 8:15), and, "Jesus is Lord" (1 Corinthians 12:3). These are the two primary prayers the Holy Spirit helps us to shout in our struggles. Then He helps us to know what to pray for and how to articulate our prayers.

THE QUESTION THE HOLY SPIRIT ASKS AND ANSWERS

The Holy Spirit wants our response to all that He's helped us to consider. The question He articulated through Paul to call for a response from the Christians in Rome is now His personal question to you and me. Allow me to reword Romans 8:31-32 as the Holy Spirit's direct question to each of us. "What then will *you* say to these things? If God is for you, who can be against you? He Who did not spare His own Son, but delivered Him up for you, how shall He not with Him freely give you all things?"

Note the difference between "these things" and "all things." Our struggles are the "these things." Then in contrast is "all things." In the Greek the phrase "all things" has an article. It should read, "the all things." In our struggles we need to remember *the* all things. What are they? Our predestined election, our call, our justification, our ever increasing glorification of being made in the likeness of Christ.

Now in the light of that, we can expect that if God didn't spare His Son, He won't spare the blessings of being a new creature in Him. He'll be with us through the Holy Spirit, assuring us of His love and answers to the prayers He guides us to pray. The Spirit helps us to pray and He prays through us. A best part of "the all things" is to live with the Father forever. The greatest Counselor in the world is prepared to be sure we make it.

5 ⟨ The Spirit of Faith

ETWEEN MY THUMB and my forefinger I'm holding one of the
smallest seeds in the world.

Now that may not be the most exciting topic sentence of a
chapter you've ever read, but stay with me. In this little seed,
Jesus tells us, is the might of the minuscule, the promise that
out of little beginnings can come great results.

I'm holding a mustard seed. Jesus said that if you and I
have faith even as small as a little speck of a seed like this,
magnificent things can happen.

Jesus' parable of the mustard seed is really a parable of how
the Holy Spirit works in us. I think the Master was looking
ahead to the post-Pentecost Age when the Holy Spirit would
be the implanter, cultivator, and nourisher of the seed of faith.

Christ, the risen, ever living Son of God, our Savior and
Lord, is the focus of faith. But He does not reveal Himself. As
A.J. Gordon said it so clearly,

Each person of the Trinity reveals another. The Son reveals
the Father, but His own revelation awaits the testimony of

the Holy Spirit.... What we need then is the Son of God, revealed in all His radiant beauty through the ministry of the Holy Spirit.... When the disciples sought to know the Father, the Lord said, "he who has seen me has seen the Father. It is His glory that shines on my face and His purpose that is fulfilled in my ministry." So the blessed Paraclete desires to turn our thought and attention to Christ, one with Him in the Holy Trinity and one He has come to reveal.[1]

∽

Like the "grace for grace" we receive through Christ (John 1:16) or multiplied grace, so too faith in response grows as we move from the primary seed of faith with which we began the Christian life to a powerful faith that grows greater and stronger.

∽

Faith is a gift of the Holy Spirit. He gives us faith in two dimensions: Faith that saves, "No one can say that Jesus is Lord except by the Holy Spirit" (1 Corinthians 12:3); and faith that sustains, "Faith by the same Spirit" (1 Corinthians 12:9). The Holy Spirit instigates in us both initiative faith and inspiring faith. A faith that claims our adoption and a faith that makes us audacious. Paul speaks of going from "faith to faith" (Romans 1:17). Like the "grace for grace" we receive through Christ (John 1:16) or multiplied grace, so too faith in response grows as we move from the primary seed of faith with which we began the Christian life to a powerful faith that grows greater and stronger.

CONFUSED CONFESSIONS

Our statements about our need for more faith expose our confusion about the source and substance of faith. "What I need to have is faith!" we say as we confront our problems. We imply that we produce the faith that's needed. Or we say, "If I only had more faith," suggesting that it's the quantity of faith that we amass that will bring results. Again for emphasis: the Holy Spirit is the source of the gift of faith in Christ and what He can do in our problems or perplexities. But there's an even greater secret to be discovered.

By far the most confusing advice some people give us is, "You don't need more faith, you need to find more of the Holy Spirit to give you that faith you need." That suggests that the Holy Spirit is illusive, a hidden mystery we must solve, the missing piece of a puzzle we must find. Our need is not just to get more of the Holy Spirit. His fullness already is penetrating our minds. *Our great need is to allow the Holy Spirit to have control of more of us!* Then we can realize the secret of dynamic living: the Holy Spirit Himself engenders the gift of faith. Our desire to receive the gift of faith without the Giver is an indication that we're still in control and want to add the gift of faith as one of our resources for our own management of life, people, and situations. True humility is to acknowledge that apart from the Holy Spirit we may wish, yearn, long, and plan, but genuine trust, authentic faith, is experienced only in union with the Holy Spirit Himself.

THE PARABLE OF THE HOLY SPIRIT

Now we can look at the parable of the mustard seed in the three ways it is presented in the Gospels. Putting them in the following order gives us a basis for a progression of thought about how the seed of the Holy Spirit Who is faith grows within us. Remember, a parable has one salient thrust, one truth to be grasped.

Note first, Matthew 13:31-32: "Another parable He put forth to them, saying: 'The kingdom of heaven is like a mustard seed, which a man took and sowed in his field, which indeed is the least of all the seeds; but when it is grown, it is greater than the herbs and becomes a tree, so that the birds of the air come and nest in its branches.'"

Now look at Matthew 17:20: "For assuredly, I say to you, if you have faith as a mustard seed, you will say to this mountain, 'Move from here to there,' and it will move; and nothing will be impossible for you."

And then in Luke 17:6 note the same reference to the mustard seed faith, "If you had faith as a mustard seed, you might say to this mulberry tree, 'Be pulled up by the roots and be planted in the sea,' and it would obey you."

Each of these variations on the theme of growth of faith in us as a result of our union with the Holy Spirit has a particular emphasis. Let's consider each of them.

The kingdom of heaven. The kingdom of heaven or the kingdom of God is the reign and rule of God in our lives. Jesus said the kingdom is to be within us, between us and others, lived in every situation, and extended to every realm of society. It must begin within us before we can impact our relationships and the world. And it all begins when the Holy Spirit speaks the word of faith through us, "Jesus is Lord." It is the Holy Spirit responding to the Son in our minds.

~

The Holy Spirit must peel back the fingers of our tenacious grip until we let go completely.

~

It may seem like a faint whisper of faith at first. It is the first easing of our tight grip on our lives. Then the Holy Spirit must peel back the fingers of our tenacious grip until we let go completely. As we are given the power to release every aspect of our minds, emotions, and wills, the reign of the Lord grows within us. The same thing happens with our relationships and responsibilities. The Holy Spirit presses on with persistence, giving us the freedom to yield and then the joy of claiming Christ as Lord. The process never ends.

In this use of the mustard seed as a similitude, the emphasis is on the growth of the kingdom. A mustard seed can produce a twelve-foot tree in which birds can nest. The growth of the kingdom did have what seemed like a small beginning in the life and message of Jesus. But after the resurrection and Pentecost, the missionary expansion reached out to the then-known world. And it's still growing today.

A minuscule beginning and mighty results. The emphasis in the Matthew 17:20 reference to faith, the size of a mustard seed that can move mountains, needs careful analysis. Here the emphasis is on the minuscule size of the faith and the mighty result. Nowhere in the parable does Jesus talk about a growing faith. Just the opposite: the faith is tiny; the moving of the mountain is tremendous. Nowhere does Jesus challenge us to increase our faith. This was the plea of the disciples, "Master, increase our faith!" Did they want a greater faith, so it could be the reason that great things would happen? Jesus simply challenged them to have faith in God. When He did commend great faith in the case of the Centurion (Matthew 8:10) and the Gentile woman who persisted in her plea for healing (Matthew 15:28), it was not the quantity but the authentic quality of complete trust in Him. When Jesus said, "Your faith has made you well," to people He healed, He was acknowledging the evidence of faith, not the magnitude of it. On the whole the Lord was alarmed at the lack of faith in people, especially His close followers, and envisioned the time when after the crucifixion and the effusion of the Holy Spirit, faith in Him as the triumphant Savior and reigning Lord would be engendered.

The clear conviction of the early church was that Christ was the only Mediator between God and humankind and that the

Holy Spirit motivated the gift of faith in Him. *Solo fide*, "by faith alone," became the message of how to be justified with God. Not the law or good works, but faith. In the same breath, Paul was quick to clarify that the faith that alone could please God was His own provision through the Holy Spirit. "For by grace you have been saved through faith, and that not of yourselves; it is the gift of God, not of works lest anyone should boast" (Ephesians 2:8).

~

The Holy Spirit, the greatest Counselor, is seeking to help us identify our mountain and pray with confidence for it to be removed, so we can move on in glorifying and serving Christ our Lord.

~

So we never look back on our conversion or on any event in which magnificent things happened and say, "My tremendous faith did it!" but rather, "Praise the Lord! He has done great things. It was not the size of my faith but the immensity of His power that did it!" The Holy Spirit gives us the vision of what the Lord wants in a situation and gives us the power of faith. He can and will do it in His own way and timing.

Most of all, He moves mountains. We all have mountains that are obstructions to our progress in discipleship or in pressing on toward the clear goals the Lord has given us. It's interesting that rabbis were called "mountain removers." Their teaching was to remove the mountains of misconceptions and of doubt.

The Holy Spirit, the greatest Counselor, is seeking to help us identify our mountain and pray with confidence for it to be removed, so we can move on in glorifying and serving Christ our Lord. It's not how great our faith is but how great is His mountain-removing power.

Unforgiven mulberry tree. The metaphor of the mustard seed remains the same in the Luke 17:6 rendering of Jesus' parable, but what is to be removed changes. How can faith the size of a mustard seed say to a mulberry tree, "Be pulled up by the roots and planted in the sea?" "Mountains I can understand, but what does the mulberry tree represent?" you say.

Consider the context. Jesus has just given an awesome challenge to forgive. "If he [your brother] sins against you seven times in a day and seven times in a day returns to you saying, 'I repent,' you shall forgive him" (Luke 17:4). We sense the Master is pressing His disciples, and us, to place no limits on our forgiveness. We remember Peter's question, "'Lord, how often shall my brother sin against me, and I forgive him? Up to seven times?' Jesus said to him, 'I do not say to you, up to seven times, but up to seventy times seven'" (Matthew 18:21). In my arithmetic that's four hundred ninety times! The Hebraism seventy times seven, rooted back in Genesis 4:24, came to mean the absence of limit. Jesus was talking about unlimited forgiveness.

No wonder the disciples said, "Increase our faith," in answer to Jesus' mandate. It was in response to this consternation that Jesus used the mustard similitude in Luke's version of the parable. Here the mulberry tree represents unforgiven hurts and offenses. And who doesn't have a grove filled with that kind of mulberry tree?

~

The Holy Spirit knows how perilous it is for us to carry the burden of unforgiven slights and oversights, hurts and harms, as well as malicious words and actions that amount to character assassination of someone we dislike.

~

Again our Counselor, the Holy Spirit, helps us identify people we need to forgive. For very good reason. Remember His responsibility to bring to our remembrance what Christ said. The only sentence in the Lord's Prayer Christ went back over for emphasis was, "Forgive us our debts as we forgive our debtors." He said, "For if you forgive men their trespasses, your heavenly Father will also forgive you. But if you do not forgive men their trespasses, neither will your Father forgive your trespasses" (Matthew 6:14-15).

The Holy Spirit knows how perilous it is for us to carry the burden of unforgiven slights and oversights, hurts and harms, as well as malicious words and actions that amount to character assassination of someone we dislike. But some of the wrongs we feel people have done to us are deeply rooted, like the roots of a tall mulberry tree. How can we pull up the tangled, spreading roots of bitter memories?

We can't. That is, we can't by ourselves. However, when we get a thorough spiritual check-up with our Counselor, He brings to our attention what unforgiveness is doing to us, let alone the person who needs to be forgiven. I'm always deeply moved when I sense the Holy Spirit express profound concern. "Lloyd, I love you too much to let you carry this unforgiven memory one more day. You must forgive or your ability to receive forgiveness will be jeopardized."

Again the old question arises, "Do I have enough faith?" or another one of those "if onlys"—"If only I had more faith, I could be that forgiving." You know the response to that! "Since when was the size of your faith the qualification for a miracle?" the Counselor asks. As long as I express my inadequacy and the least bit of willingness to picture what it would be like to be free, the Holy Spirit helps me bring the hurt to the cross. The longer the memory has been rooted, the greater the miracle. And it's not dependent on a great deal of faith but trust in a great Savior to Whom the Holy Spirit constantly leads me.

The tiny mustard seed is still between the forefinger and thumb of my right hand, while as a lefty I have hand-written this chapter. It's so small! Like our faith—a gift in union with the Holy Spirit. It can never be ours without Him. But with it empowered by Him, the floodgates for the flow of limitless power open!

6 ⟩ Abounding in Hope

I N HIS BENCHMARK BOOK ON HOPE, *The Theology of Hope,* German theologian Jurgen Moltmann makes the vital link between the faith we talked about in the previous chapter and the empowering of hope:

> Thus, in the Christian life faith has the priority, but hope the primacy. Without faith's knowledge of Christ, hope becomes a utopia and remains hanging in the air. But without hope, faith falls to pieces, becomes faint-hearted and ultimately a dead faith. It is through faith that a person finds the path of true life, but it is only hope that keeps him on that path. Thus it is that faith in Christ gives hope its assurance. Thus it is that hope gives faith in Christ its breadth and leads it into life![1]

So straightaway let's go to the salient point I want to communicate in this chapter about the Holy Spirit as our Counselor. Just as true faith is engendered in us by Him, the Holy Spirit *enables* authentic hope. He doesn't just give hope. He *is* the source of abounding hope within us.

It's best not to turn that assertion around and suggest that what we call hope always is the Holy Spirit. There are too many facsimiles of hope around to trifle with that idea.

Human perceptions of what hope is usually involve wishful thinking. We all have wishes for ourselves, for other people, and for the future. These wishes are the result of our human desires— what we have evaluated would be best for us and others, or for some situation. Sometimes we try to wish things into existence. At the same time, we attempt to wish away other things.

Another facsimile of authentic hope is yearning. We incorrectly use the word hope to express this longing. Our daily expressions, "Well, I hope so!" or, "Here's hoping" or, "Where there's life there's hope!" are rooted in our humanly induced yearning. It is an intensified brand of wishing. We try to make things happen by yearning them into being.

This yearning sometimes masquerades for prayer. Winston Churchill said, "We build our houses and then our houses build us." In the same way we draft our castles in the air according to our specifications and then yearn for God to help us build them. Often we are disappointed when He doesn't build the castles of our dreams on time, or when He has other plans for what is best for us.

∾

Our daily expressions, "Well, I hope so!" or, "Here's hoping" or, "Where there's life there's hope!" are rooted in our humanly induced yearning. It is an intensified brand of wishing. We try to make things happen by yearning them into being.

∾

Optimism is another bogus substitute for genuine hope. Richard Rodgers' song from *South Pacific,* sung with such gusto by the late Mary Martin, began, "I'm only a cockeyed optimist." Lots of what we call optimism is cockeyed. Optimism and hope are confused so often. Creative optimism is a by-product of something more than a happy disposition. There are people who have what seems to be an optimistic personality because of their conditioning and experience. However, unless optimism is based on something more solid, often the optimist sets himself or herself up for big disappointments. I've lived through the fires of difficulty with too many ungrounded optimists to suggest that optimism alone lasts for the long pull when the going gets really rough.

"Well," you say, "if hope isn't wishing or yearning or surface optimism, what is it?"

A TRIPLE-BRAIDED CORD

Authentic "hope" is a triple-braided cord. One of the two main Hebrew words for hope in the Old Testament has its root meaning as "cord" or "rope." Building on that image, for me true hope has three strands that are braided together. You'll not be surprised when I suggest that those strands come from the Persons of the Trinity.

The first strand is woven of the enduring fabric of the faithfulness of the Father, His righteousness, mercy, and the reliability of His promises.

The second strand of the cord of hope is Christ and His fulfillment of God's promises. Credible hope is based on the historical fact of the Incarnation of the Messiah, in the Person of Jesus of Nazareth. In Him, the kingdom of God, His reign and rule, has been established. Christ's life, message, atonement for the sins of the world, and especially His resurrection in time are now the basis of hope in our time. Christ is the object of our hope.

The Holy Spirit is the third strand of lasting hope. One

with the Father and the Son, the Holy Spirit could be called the Spirit of hope. When He seals us and we keep on allowing Him to fill us, hope is engendered in us through His indwelling presence.

It may be difficult for some to think of hope as a manifestation of the indwelling power of the Holy Spirit. We are so used to thinking of hope as something we must produce. When we experience uncertain and difficult times, we search within ourselves to try to conjure up hope. Often we place our expectations on what someone can do for us or some magic reversal of disturbing circumstances. In tough times, I've found that asking the Holy Spirit for hope has wonderful results. He actually produces the hope I could not develop on my own. He reminds me of the Father's faithfulness and leads me back to Calvary and the empty tomb. He gives me fresh confidence to trust the future to my reigning Lord and Savior. It's then that I can affirm the triple-braided cord and sing with hymn writer James Small:

> He drew me with the cords of love
> And thus He drew me to Him.
> And 'round my heart still closely twine
> Those ties which can't be severed.
> For I am His, and He is mine,
> Forever and forever.[2]

ABOUNDING IN HOPE

There was never any confusion about the substance and source of Paul's hope. His benedictory words to the Romans attest to that: "Now may the God of hope fill you with all joy and peace in believing, that you may abound in hope *through the power of the Holy Spirit*" (Romans 15:13, emphasis mine). The Holy Spirit produced the joy and peace in the apostle by being the Spirit of faith in him, and He was no less the Spirit of hope that surged in his being. Paul did not become the fearless, indefatigable apostle of hope only because of the facts on which his theology was built, or even because of his cherished memory of his encounter with the living Christ on the Damascus road, but because he followed his own advice to constantly keep on being filled with the Holy Spirit. He was one of the most hopeful people who ever lived precisely because he abounded in hope *by* the power of the Holy Spirit.

~

In tough times, I've found that asking the Holy Spirit for hope has wonderful results. He actually produces the hope I could not develop on my own.

~

The Greek word "abound" flashes like a diamond before us. It is *perisseúein* from the verb *perisseuō*, meaning abundance in an overflowing quantity, limitless in measure, and furnished from an artesian supply. You and I can abound in this hope when the Holy Spirit flows into, in, and through us.

Paul's heartening words to the Romans about authentic hope can become very personal for us if we pray them in the first person singular. "Now I pray that the God of hope will fill me with all joy and peace in believing, that I may abound in hope through the power of the Holy Spirit."

HOPE THROUGH THE SPIRIT OF HOPE

This prayer can begin our daily counseling session with the Holy Spirit. It initiates a conversation that continues through the day. We need a fresh supply of abounding hope to face the abrasive demands of life. I can't remember any day since I became a counselee of the greatest Counselor that there wasn't some relationship, problem, or challenging opportunity in which I needed hope.

The wishings, yearnings, and self-induced optimism I mentioned earlier just won't do—nor will placing my expectations on people, or the idea that eventually things work out, or the shibboleth that "time heals everything." I need a daily tonic of hope to fire my blood, clear my mind, and impel my will. Time alone with the Holy Spirit to talk out my worries and fears, uncertainties and complexities, as well as my need for clarity and vision, has now become an absolute necessity. I need the perspective of the Lord's plans for me as the context of hope, coupled with a fresh draught of hope from the Holy Spirit Himself. Coming to know the Holy Spirit as the Spirit of hope has revolutionized my life. I used to pray for hope thinking I could run off in my own direction to use it to keep me stabilized in the rough and tumble of a demanding schedule. Now I know that lasting hope is a by-product of consistent communion with the Holy Spirit.

~

Experiences in which the Holy Spirit has given us hope build up what I like to call a "hope memory bank."

~

Five years ago, I had a traumatic experience that vividly reminded me of how the Holy Spirit provides hope in difficult circumstances. It happened while hiking alone in a desolate place on the northwest coast of Scotland. I had hiked a long distance from the little hotel where I was staying. While climbing the gigantic rocks nature has piled up along that portion of the coast, I slipped and my left leg was caught in the vice of a cleft between the rocks. The fall knocked me unconscious.

When I awoke and pulled my leg out of the cleft of rock, I realized that it was badly crushed. I knew I could not stay there all night; I had to find a way to get to the main road. It was impossible to crawl because of the excruciating pain in my leg. The only way was to drag myself on my back using my arms and hands to inch my body off the seaside boulders and through very rugged terrain.

During the almost three-hour ordeal, I cried out for the Holy Spirit to give me strength to endure. I needed hope to sustain me when I was tempted to give up. The "Inner Voice" was more pronounced than ever before in my experience of Him as my Counselor. Through the thick fog of pain, He articulated a promise in Jeremiah 29:11 I had memorized years before, "'For I know the thoughts that I think toward you,' says the Lord, 'thoughts of peace and not of evil, to give you a future and a hope.'"

"Lloyd, you have a future and a hope!" became the cheer-leading voice of the Holy Spirit. With the "Inner Voice" sounding in my heart, I kept on dragging myself until I reached the main road and later was found and carried by ambulance to a hospital. The Holy Spirit continued to repeat the promise of hope all through a complicated surgery, three months in bed, and learning to walk again.

~

I used to pray for hope thinking I could run off in my own direction to use it to keep me stabilized in the rough and tumble of a demanding schedule. Now I know that lasting hope is a by-product of consistent communion with the Holy Spirit.

~

Now five years later, I still feel the positive impact of this experience of hope through the power of the Holy Spirit. It has made me all the more expectant for His fresh supply of hope each day.

Experiences in which the Holy Spirit has given us hope

build up what I like to call a "hope memory bank." It gives us confidence when new challenges or difficulties arise in which we need a renewed infilling of hope.

The Holy Spirit often brings back to my remembrance Christ's exchange with the Father during the final week of His incarnate ministry. As the Savior drew near to the cross He prayed, "Father, glorify Your name." The response was, "I have both glorified it and will glorify it again" (John 12:28). In each situation in which we need hope, the crucial prayer the Holy Spirit helps us express is, "Lord, glorify Your name! Your will be done! Your glory be revealed!" This prayer of relinquishment and surrender gives us freedom from worry and blesses us with profound peace. Then the Spirit sounds the words in our souls that become the basis of our hope, "I have glorified it and will glorify it again."

~

The Holy Spirit is the orchestrator of these surprises. Consistent counseling with Him makes us expectant and vibrant with hope.

~

The late James S. Stewart, one of Scotland's great scholar-preachers who was my professor of New Testament Studies at the University of Edinburgh, underlined the importance of this promise as a source of hope. "These words are dramatic assertion of one basic fact of our faith: the fact, namely, that it is God's way to go beyond the best He has done before; that therefore a living faith will always have in it a certain element of surprise and tension and discovery; that what we have seen and learned of God up to the present is not the end of our seeing nor the sum total of our learning; that whatever we have found in Christ is only a fraction of what we still can find; that the spiritual force which in the great days past vitalized the Church and shaped the course of history has not lost its energies and fallen into abeyance, but is liable at any moment to burst out anew and take control...."[3] The Holy Spirit is the orchestrator of these surprises. Consistent counseling with Him makes us expectant and vibrant with hope.

I have a friend who keeps what he calls an "Ebenezer Log Book." It's based on 1 Samuel 7:12. After a victory of Israel over the Philistines, Samuel "took a stone and set it up between Mizpah and Shen, and called its name Ebenezer saying, 'Thus far the Lord has helped us.'" My friend records the experiences in his life in which the Lord has intervened to help him in the battles of life, times when he has had to exclaim, "In this the Lord has helped me." When life gets stressful, he goes back to the Ebenezer memorial stones erected along the path of his pilgrimage. He affirms, "When I remember how I've been helped in the past, the Holy Spirit gives me a burst of hope for the future."

~

All our worries are put into the perspective that through Christ's resurrection, we are alive forever, and nothing can denigrate our destiny.

~

Life for me constantly is lived on the edge of the future. As a pastor of a large church and the leader of a national broadcast ministry, my task isn't just to solve problems, but to prayerfully envision what the Lord through the guidance of the Holy Spirit wants for the next strides into the future. When His guidance supersedes my human expectations (or reservations!), I realize that I must depend on supernatural power to pull off what the Lord has made clear. He must do it. It's on that edge especially that I've come to depend on the Holy Spirit's artesian flow of hope.

In our counseling sessions of dialogue prayer with the Holy Spirit, he helps us clarify our concerns. He reassures us of the faithfulness of the Father and Christ's overcoming power. All our worries are put into the perspective that through Christ's resurrection, we are alive forever, and nothing can denigrate our destiny. We can live with a vibrant expectation of His timely interventions because we have been resurrected out of an old life by a new birth. We can expect daily, diminutive resurrections out of the graves of worry, fear, and anxiety. In the ambience of that assurance, the Holy Spirit helps us trust our problems and perplexities to the Lord. When we do, the floodgates of our hearts are opened to the inflow of His incredible power of hope. But don't forget: it's a supernatural provision inseparable from the Provider.

We simply can't make it through any day or a lifetime with any degree of serenity without these hope-infusing counseling sessions with the Holy Spirit. We are surrounded by people devoid of His quality of hope and a pall of grim hopelessness hangs over so much of life today.

~

Many are not experiencing better days because of their lack of authentic hope. Often they are engulfed by the mood of discouragement.

~

The artist G.F. Watts painted a picture he called "Hope." There is a blindfolded woman with her head bowed and holding a lyre, sitting on a sphere, supposedly the world. Only one string of the instrument is unbroken and being plucked; only one star shines in a dark sky.

Watts wanted to interpret his painting for those who might not understand its symbolic meaning. He had the word "Hope" put on a sign placed beneath the painting when it first hung in a British art gallery.

The story goes that after hours two Cockney cleaning women stood looking at the painting. One, expressing her wonderment, said, "Hope? Now why would that be called Hope?"

"Well," the other charwoman replied, "I s'pose she's hopin' she ain't gonna fall off!"

Lots of people could project themselves into Watts' painting. With expectantly crossed fingers, they pluck the one string of vague desire for life to work out, while they long for the morning star which promises the dawn of a better day.

Many are not experiencing better days because of their lack of authentic hope. Often they are engulfed by the mood of discouragement. Sometimes they spread the contagion. Oscar Wilde captured this condition in *Reading Gaol:*

> We did not dare to breathe a prayer
> Or give our anguish scope.
> Something was dead in all of us,
> And what was dead was hope.[4]

It's in a world like ours today that we come to our Counselor for perspective and the power to hope.

LET'S BE PRACTICAL

At this point you may be saying, "Okay, Lloyd, let's be practical. Exactly how do I go about having a counseling session with the Holy Spirit about areas in my life where I need His hope?"

In response, I'd suggest a method the Holy Spirit has taught me and that has worked for many others with whom I've shared it.

To begin, block out at least an hour alone with the Holy Spirit. A longer time is even better. Some who have tried this method have taken a day away alone. The important thing, however, is to be open, be specific, write down what you learn, and then ask for hope for the needs, people, and concerns you've discussed in dialogue prayer.

Begin your session with a prayer something like this:

"Holy Spirit, I want to become a hopeful thinker about my life, my family, and my friends. I need Your inspiration to focus short and long-range hopes based on Your guidance. Draw me into intimate conversation with the triple-braided cord of the Father's faithfulness, Christ's resurrection power that makes life a constant chance of a new beginning where all things are possible, and Your power to hope that can make me an expectant, hopeful person. Anoint my mind. Cleanse my memory of anything that might limit what is possible. Control my imagination to be an instrument of forming the picture of what I should dare to hope by Your enabling Spirit. Thank you for using this time to conform me further to the image of Christ."

∾

"Holy Spirit, I want to become a hopeful thinker about my life, my family, and my friends. I need Your inspiration to focus short and long-range hopes based on Your guidance."

∾

Now take some pieces of ruled paper. Write out the following categories with space between each for what the Holy Spirit inspires you to hope. Personally, I've found a notebook even more helpful with a few pages set aside for each category. This allows space for recording further inspiration as the days go by and for the discipline of an accountability review, which I suggest in my last chapter entitled, "Check the Dailies."

A plan for prayer. Here are some areas in our lives in which the Holy Spirit wants to guide our thinking and provide the power of supernatural hope.

1. As I prayerfully think about the future of my life as a servant of Christ, where do I need to grow? What should I hope for to glorify Christ more completely?

2. In my own personal life, what is the Holy Spirit guiding me to pray for that would require His power to hope? What are the raw nerves of frustration that often get me down?

3. What should I hope by the Spirit's power for my family and friends? How can I become a better communicator of Spirit-inspired hope to them?

4. What are the troublesome problems, situations, or circumstances around me that cause worry and anxiety? What hope is the Holy Spirit encouraging me to claim by His power?

5. What should I hope for in the challenges and opportunities of my job? How can I glorify Christ more effectively in my work?

6. What is the Holy Spirit enabling me to hope for my church? What is He seeking to affirm or change? Am I in tune with His strategy? Am I doing what He wants me to do to cooperate with His plans? Do I have genuine hope for my church? Do the pastor and fellow members think of me as a hopeful visionary?

7. What about my personal ministry of caring for individuals in need and problems in my community? Am I willing and able to share my faith with those who don't know Christ? What social needs in my community are on the Lord's agenda for me? What is the Lord calling me to do? What hope do I need to press on faithfully and obediently?

The need for feedback. In addition to prayer, we all need honest feedback from the significant people in our lives. Yet their feedback is limited by what they can observe and hear. The Holy Spirit knows us absolutely and utterly. When we dare to ask Him the above questions, He answers with divine omniscience. He knows the Lord's plans for us. His task is to create in us a hope for what He inspires. More than any human loved one or friend, He is for us—never against us. He helps us refine our vision, define our goals, and design our priorities.

The one dominant hope the Holy Spirit engenders in us is to glorify Christ. When this becomes our all-encompassing hope, we can deal with times when our wishes are not fulfilled in the way we wanted. That's why it's so important to listen to the Holy Spirit's answer to those questions. His hope is given to accomplish the Lord's will, not just our projected wishes and longings.

～

The one dominant hope the Holy Spirit engenders in us is to glorify Christ. When this becomes our all-encompassing hope, we can deal with times when our wishes are not fulfilled in the way we wanted.

～

A friend of mine used these questions on a retreat alone in his cabin in the mountains. He spent a weekend writing out the answers he received. His account of what happened to him is very insightful:

I came back a different man. I have new vision for my life and greater hope for the future than I've ever had before. It made all the difference to realize that the Holy Spirit is to be my hoping power.

Strange as it may seem, the more I sought the guidance of the Holy Spirit, the more he pointed me to Christ. I was astounded by how limited was my vision in my own answers to most all of the questions. I realized that many of my desires for my life were for my personal comfort and not for serving Christ. I have some new priorities and a fresh hope that they can and will be done. But whatever happens, the Holy Spirit will use it to bring me closer to Christ. I've discovered that you've really got to let hope have you. For me, that's very different than living in response to the guilt-producing saying, "You gotta have hope!"

COMMUNICATORS OF HOPE

Really letting the Holy Spirit have us is the quantum leap into our calling to be communicators of hope to other people. We were meant to be contagious with hope. The Holy Spirit wants to make us hopeful thinkers and hopeful affirmers of others. We can't do that until we abound in hope ourselves. This happens when we see tangible results of the time we spend with our Counselor. Discouragement about ourselves is overcome when we realize the changes in our personalities He has made possible. We begin to feel hopeful about our progress and can be hopeful about what He can do in others.

~

The Spirit of hope builds a bridge over the interface between where and what we are to where and what He wants to enable us to be.

~

The questions we asked our Counselor in our "hope session" with him express our openness to change and grow. We discover some vital changes needed in our attitudes and actions. Then with a fresh infusion of hope, we dare to believe that we can be different. The Spirit of hope builds a bridge over the interface between where and what we are to where and what He wants to enable us to be.

A woman who is trusting the Holy Spirit as her Counselor had this to say after her "hope inventory" with Him:

That deep time with the Holy Spirit really challenged those five discouraging words, "It won't make any difference." I had been debilitated with these vandalizing words. They kept me on dead center (an awful place to be!) for years. With these words I poured cold water on my own potential and my desire to help people or do anything in the community. It wasn't hard to find others who agreed that whatever you do, it won't make any difference. That's the motto of most people today. But now I've begun to live with a different five-word motto: "Hope makes all the difference!"

One of the most exciting things I see happening to people who allow the Holy Spirit to replenish them with abounding hope daily is their involvement in community problems. People with Holy Spirit-inspired hope in Christ no longer buy into the idea that whatever they try won't make any difference. In fact, they are making a difference by feeding the hungry, caring for the homeless, working to rebuild Los Angeles, battling for justice in racial issues, and helping the disadvantaged.

∿

People find it difficult to resist conversations opened by a caring question like, "How are you doing these days? Are you feeling hopeful about the future?"

∿

These communicators of hope have an indomitable conviction expressed in four "Rs"—people can be rescued, redeemed, rehabilitated, and returned to society as new men and women.

I've also noticed that those who have taken the hope inventory with the greatest Counselor and have followed it up with daily renewal of His hope have become much freer and genuine in their willingness to talk to unbelievers and nominal church members about Christ. It's not surprising that hope has been the key to opening deep conversations about the Christian life.

People find it difficult to resist conversations opened by a caring question like, "How are you doing these days? Are you feeling hopeful about the future?" Talk about conditions in the world soon is turned to more personal issues. The door of opportunity usually opens when an authentic communicator of hope says, "I've had an amazing experience of real hope recently. Sometime I'd like to tell you about it."

So often the other person's reply is, "Why not now for openers?" Hope can be the lead into unstudied, nonpious, down-to-earth conversation. It becomes a three-way conversation: the Holy Spirit is there feeding His communicator of hope with the right lines!

The greatest Counselor in the world is always ready to answer our prayer asking for His help, as Amy Carmichael beautifully expressed in a poem:

> Hope through me, God of Hope
> Or never can I know
> Deep wells and loving streams of Hope,
> And pools of overflow.
> O blessed Hope of God,
> Flow through me patiently,
> Until I hope for everyone
> As You have hoped for me.[5]

Now here's a helpful guide for a daily update with our Counselor: How has being empowered with the Spirit of hope changed my thinking, attitudes, and actions? How am I feeling about the future? Is hope beginning to abound in my relationships? In which relationship is it most challenging to be a hopeful thinker and affirmer? Why? What does the Holy Spirit counsel about that? Has the power of hope instigated positive new confidence in being a communicator of hope at work, in the community, with people who are tired of wishing and longing and whose optimism has run out? If I threw caution to the wind, what would I do today to express the hope I've received?

At the end of a current review like that, ask for and accept your supply of abounding hope for the day. Abound in hope today and every day for the rest of your life.

7 } Love Has No Write-Offs

"**L**LOYD, MY BROTHER, this is the body of the Lord Jesus Christ *broken for you.... This is the blood of Christ *shed for you.*"

These traditional words, drenched with love and caring, were spoken to me by Fred Grayston, an elder in my church, as he served me the sacred elements at a Communion Service recently. Fred's emphasis on "for you!" was unmistakable.

I was deeply moved. Suddenly, I began to sob. My body shook with intensity as what felt like liquid love washed over me and then surged within me. The flow continued for the next fifteen minutes as Fred and the other elders served Communion to the congregation.

There I sat behind the Communion Table in front of thirteen hundred people with tears streaming down my face. The pastors seated on both sides of me gripped my arms. They sensed that something very profound was going on inside of me.

Indeed, it was. The Communion of the Holy Spirit was

happening. I shouldn't have been surprised. I had just preached a Communion meditation on the power of the Holy Spirit to make the grace of Christ and the love of God intensely personal. The promise I had held out to the congregation was fulfilled in my own heart. I was stunned again by the immensity of God's limitless love and the magnitude of Christ's sacrifice on the cross. The Holy Spirit had broken through to a deeper level of my heart and filled me with incredible love. Joy pulsated within me; then an awesome peace pervaded my mind and emotions as I closed the service.

The thrilling thing was that what happened to me also happened to many others that day. A fresh anointing by the Holy Spirit was graciously given us. Tears of joy glistened on faces throughout the sanctuary.

Those who spoke with me after the service shared a similar experience of being overcome with the depth of love communicated by the Holy Spirit. All of the people with whom I talked confided some challenging relationship in which extraordinary love was needed from them. We all agreed that the outpouring of love was perfectly timed for our church.

～

A fresh anointing by the Holy Spirit was graciously given us. Tears of joy glistened on faces throughout the sanctuary.

～

It was World Communion Sunday, a day when we reaffirm our unity in diversity as an interracial, intercultural, intergenerational church. In preparation for Communion, people from many different national and ethnic backgrounds had prayed in their native tongue for our church as it faces the needs of our city. The gift of love through the Holy Spirit had not been given in a vacuum. It was provided for a church recommitted to oneness in Christ, and to those who longed for a greater measure of supernatural love for their personal ministries of caring for others.

The Holy Spirit wants to pour love into our hearts, not just in special outpourings like I've described, but daily in our counseling sessions with Him in prayer. He is ever ready to help us when we admit our need to love profoundly even those who are difficult to love, who get on our nerves or stretch our patience to the breaking point when we'd just as soon write them off.

THE HOLY SPIRIT'S BIG ASSIGNMENT

One of the biggest assignments of the Holy Spirit, our Counselor, is to implement through us Christ's awesome mission statement for us. "A new commandment I give to you, that you love one another; as I have loved you, that you also love one another. By this all will know that you are my disciples, if you have love for one another" (John 13:34-35).

∼

The Holy Spirit is Love. Love is the primary fruit of the Spirit. He is the love that is required to live out Jesus' new commandment to love others as He has loved us.

∼

The Holy Spirit seeks to be in us the love that Jesus defined. He engenders faith to believe in Christ as Lord and Savior, empowers us with hope, *and* actually endues us with a power to love way beyond our human ability.

The Holy Spirit is Love. Love is the primary fruit of the Spirit. He *is* the love that is required to live out Jesus' new commandment to love others as He has loved us.

Okay for openers. Now take a look at the raw recruits the Holy Spirit is assigned to train in what it means to love.

People like you and me! Think of the tough time we have loving as Christ has loved us. We're still in basic training when it comes to the issues of unqualified love for those we tend to consider unworthy people. We wrestle with condemnatory judgments. We often find it difficult to forgive and struggle to forget the hurting memories of what people have said or done to us. And serving others as Christ's servants? Love the way Jesus loved? Too much for the likes of us without the empowering love of the Holy Spirit.

~

The Holy Spirit is very concerned about what's in your spirit and mine. He wants to dwell there. He knows the stakes are high.

~

But the Holy Spirit is no grim, imperious drill sergeant in training us. He is our Counselor; He accepts us right where we are in our problems with loving ourselves and others; He provides the love to do and be what Christ's new commandment demands. To do that He persistently draws us back to what Christ said about the love He requires in His disciples.

Rather than dealing with the general theme of love in this chapter, I sense the Holy Spirit wants us to confront one of the most crippling problems we face in allowing Him to love through us. It's a problem we all have. Simply put, it's the problem of negative criticism that grows into the habit of being hypercritical and results in a censorious spirit.

The Holy Spirit is very concerned about what's in your spirit and mine. He wants to dwell there. He knows the stakes are high. He is assigned to help us grapple with Christ's challenge that confronts this big problem blocking us from receiving and communicating the love required by the commandment to love. "Judge not, that you be not judged," the Holy Spirit reminds us, echoing Christ, "for with what judgment you judge, you will be judged; and with the same measure you use, it will be measured back to you" (Matthew 7:1-2).

In an extended time with our Counselor about our calling to love, He asks us to open our relational ledgers. He keeps auditing mine. He also may want to go over yours with you. Perhaps this chapter can be that for both of us. I think He wants us to take a good look at our relational write-offs.

PEOPLE WRITE-OFFS

In our day of income tax returns, deductible contributions, and ledgers of profit and loss, we all know about write-offs. In precise definition, a write-off is a cancellation, an amount canceled and noted as a loss.

The term write-off is also used relationally for writing off a person. There are people we've canceled out in our minds long before our attitudes or involvement with them sends a termination notice. Our love, caring, and concern is cut off.

~

He wants us to understand that writing off another person, without ever coming to a place of seeking or expressing forgiveness, puts us in the perilous position of being written off by God!

~

Just the other day I met an old friend on a cross-country flight. Quite naturally, we began to play catch-up with each other. That led to a conversation about mutual friends we had known in the past. In the course of this reflection, I mentioned a man whom I thought was one of his best friends. I was shocked by his response.

"Listen, I have written that guy off. He's yesterday! He's canceled from my list of friends. If I never see him again, it will be too soon!"

My friend then proceeded to tell me what was wrong with the man's beliefs, politics, behavior, and most of all, his failure to measure up as a friend when he had needed him. Criticism had turned to cynicism and cynicism to censoriousness. And my friend is a Christian! His relationship with God was in jeopardy.

Ever felt the way this man did? Have you any write-offs? The Holy Spirit knows and is especially concerned about those we harbor in our thinking. He wants us to understand that writing off another person, without ever coming to a place of seeking or expressing forgiveness, puts us in the perilous position of being written off by God!

"Now wait a minute!" you say. "Doesn't God love us regardless of what we do or say? Doesn't faith in Christ assure us of a relationship with God in spite of our attitudes or behavior?"

The Holy Spirit's response is to remind us of what we should and should not write off. So the title of this chapter, "Love Has No Write-Offs," is only half-true. Love never cancels people, but it should cancel from our ledger of memory what some of them have done or said that harmed or hurt us. And if we don't?

I sense that the Holy Spirit allows us to dangle over the abyss of that frightening danger as He guides our thinking about Christ's bracing prohibition not to judge that we be not judged. In that position, we are to consider what the Lord meant when He told us that we would be judged with the same judgment with which we've judged others. The Holy Spirit is most concerned that we grapple with the fact that the measure of love we will be capable of receiving from Him is directly related to our willingness to let Him love through us.

Now the Holy Spirit has our attention! This counseling session with Him has taken an unexpected turn; it cannot be otherwise. Christ's absolute about judging stands. The Holy Spirit does not water it down. Instead, He helps us think it through and then offers us the power to do something about our people write-offs.

WHAT CHRIST MEANT

What did Christ really mean in this hard saying about judging? Aren't we to use our God-given faculties of evaluation and critical analysis? Who can ever completely be free of judging people and their actions? In response, the Holy Spirit guides our study of the Lord's command.

In the Greek, "Judge not," *me krinete* is a prohibition in the present imperative of the verb *krinō*. It means, "Do not keep on judging! Don't make a habit of judging others." The verb *krinō* has three uses.

The first is to judge judicially, as in a court of law. Surely Jesus is not abolishing law and order. We must reject Tolstoy's idea, based on this verse, that "Christ totally forbids the human institution of any law court and that he could mean nothing else by these words." Jesus is not talking about judges in law courts, but about our responsibility with one another.

The second use of the verb *krinō* means to discern critically. Again, we are confident that Jesus is not admonishing us to dispense or suspend our analytical gifts of discernment. Nor would the Holy Spirit who dispenses those gifts mean that. Moral judgments of right and wrong about ourselves and others are not to be discarded.

The third use of *krinō* is what Jesus is talking about. His warning is against condemnatory judgments. We are not to presume God's authority by setting ourselves up as judges of the ultimate worth of another person. The psalmist prayed a model prayer to overcome this proclivity, "Keep back Your servant from presumptuous sins; Let them not have dominion over me" (Psalm 19:13). The greatest presumption is to play God in a judgment of a person that makes us think we are justified in writing off him or her. It is not our prerogative to pronounce judgment in the final sense.

~

We never forget that we are sinners saved by grace alone (Ephesians 2:8). Righteous judgments are saturated with the grace we've received.

~

The Holy Spirit underlines another of Christ's statements about judging to help us understand how and how not to judge. "Do not judge according to appearance, but judge with righteous judgment" (John 7:24). Righteous judgments have several important ingredients. They are made out of a right relationship with the Lord and done with an awareness of our own failures and shortcomings. We never forget that we are sinners saved by grace alone (Ephesians 2:8). Righteous judgments are saturated with the grace we've received. They are made with love that cannot be broken. Also they are made on the basis of the Lord's standards of righteousness.

The Holy Spirit does not counsel us to have a flabby, indulgent attitude. Nor does He encourage us to buy into our age of appeasement and tolerance where everything is relative and there are no absolutes. However, the Holy Spirit shows us that any judgment of people's infractions of these absolutes must be done with indefatigable love and a willingness to help them. Affirmation of people does not have to mean advocacy for their wrongful lifestyle or behavior. That's a tightrope to balance on. That's why we need the Holy Spirit's help.

Two years ago a man who is a lay leader in my congregation drifted into an immoral sexual relationship. The pastors and elders had to pray for the Holy Spirit to guide their confrontation of the man, but also for a program of remedial rehabilitation. A righteous judgment had to be made. He was excluded from active leadership for an extended period while he received spiritual and psychological help, but he never was written off. During this period, he returned to his wife and together they worked hard to build a new marriage. Today he's back in active leadership.

It's a constant challenge for any church not to become a house of condemnatory judgment in which our wounded are spiritually executed by a firing squad of merciless fellow members. Jesus said the world will know that we are His disciples by the way we love one another. This includes the world's evaluation not only of our talk about love, but also how we deal with members and leaders who fail. Lots of nonbelievers in the world have an acute sense of their inadequacies and culpability and are turned off when they see Christians who are unwilling to couple confrontation with remedial love and forgiveness. Honesty prompts all of us to remember times we have shown the world so much less than an authentic example of Jesus' new commandment.

GOING DEEPER

So, let's allow the Holy Spirit to take us deeper. He knows that our condemnatory write-offs of people block His gift of love. He is in charge of measuring out His love in proportion to our willingness to communicate noncondemnatory love for others. So, if we are stingy lovers, He must lead us into a much more profound experience of the Lord's love for us. We can express only what we've experienced, but if the love we've received is withheld from others, our ability to continue to receive is debilitated.

At this point in our counseling with the Holy Spirit, He teaches us what's really *new* about Jesus' new commandment. It goes beyond Leviticus 19:18, "You shall love your neighbor as yourself." This verse has been the basis of the theory that we can't really love our neighbor until we love ourselves. It is both spiritually and psychologically sound that healthy love for ourselves is essential to being open to communicate love to others.

However, the new aspect of Jesus' commandment is that we need to love as He has loved us. So mere self-love is not the standard, but Christ's love is. Simply loving ourselves does not motivate us to love others. Christ's giving, forgiving, sacrificial love that has no limits and is revealed in the cross must be the motivation of the creative self-esteem that enables us to communicate noncondemnatory love.

~

The new aspect of Jesus' commandment is that we need to love as He has loved us. So mere self-love is not the standard, but Christ's love is.

~

There's so much talk about self-esteem these days, it's easy to confuse it with subtle pride or self-aggrandizement. True self-esteem is not simply having a good impression of ourselves; we know too much about our mistakes and failures. Nor is self-esteem only the result of the affirmation and accolades of other people. And self-esteem is not just the outgrowth of a successful life by human standards; some very successful people are driven by the insecurity of low self-esteem.

Authentic self-esteem is confidence in our worth. That must come from something greater than our view of our talents, physical attractiveness, or intellectual prowess. It must exceed the value other people put on us or our performance. Profound self-esteem is confidence in our worth to God. We look at the cross and exclaim, "Christ died for me! That's how much I'm worth to God!" To refuse to accept, affirm, and cherish—yes, love—ourselves as loved by God through Christ is blasphemy. It's contradicting God's estimate of our value. Self-esteem is really letting God love us.

Getting our thinking straight. The Holy Spirit takes us back to a passage He inspired Paul to write about how we receive this quality of love. In Romans 5:1-5 we are given a guide for understanding how love happens in us:

> Therefore, having been justified by faith, we have peace with God through our Lord Jesus Christ, through whom we also have access by faith into this grace in which we stand, and rejoice in hope of the glory of God. And not only that, but we also glory in tribulations, knowing that tribulation produces perseverance; and perseverance, character; and character, hope. And hope does not disappoint, because the *love of God has been poured out in our hearts by the Holy Spirit who was given to us* (emphasis mine).

Don't miss the progression. The Holy Spirit points us to Christ's revelation of the love of God and instigates faith to accept it. He produces hope in our character so we can persevere in tribulations (most of which are caused by people), and actually pours this love into our hearts. Christ is the Mediator of God's love, and the Holy Spirit is the manifestation of that love in our hearts. This is the awesome measure of love the Holy Spirit seeks to measure out in us, enabling us to love as Christ has loved us.

Amazing love. Next the Holy Spirit leads us to another passage He inspired Paul to write. First Corinthians, chapter thirteen, is really a description of the love Christ defined and the love He reproduces in us through the Holy Spirit.

Our Counselor helps us to read this chapter on love in two ways. First, He asks us to read verses 4-8 putting the name of Christ in place of the word "love." This helps us grasp how Christ loves us. Then the Holy Spirit encourages us to read the passage using the pronoun "I" in place of the word "love." Through the love He pours into our hearts, we should be able to say a paraphrase something like this: "I suffer long and am kind, I do not envy; I do not parade myself, I am not puffed up, I do not behave rudely, I do not demand my way, I am not easily provoked, thinking no evil or rejoicing in other people's iniquity, but I rejoice in the truth. I bear all things, believe all things, hope all things and endure all things. This love the Holy Spirit has poured into my heart will never fail."

I have to admit that I had a hard time when the Holy Spirit first gave me this vision of the quality of love he wants to pour into my heart. It made me realize what measure of love was available and how little I'd allowed Him to equip me with His abundance of love. In that light, I could begin to consider what He revealed love is not. This made me see times when the lack of His measure of love made me envious, puffed up with pretension, rude, self-centered, edgy, and judgmental of others.

~

I have to admit that I had a hard time when the Holy Spirit first gave me this vision of the quality of love he wants to pour into my heart.

~

Using this chapter to allow our Counselor to show us how we are doing as receivers and communicators of love gets our conversation with Him out of a nebulous, conceptual realm into reality. It also frees us from comparing our level of loving with how others love. Sometimes when we evaluate our ability to love in comparison with someone we think excels at loving, we are intimidated. Equally ineffective is the fake confidence that we luxuriate in when we compare ourselves with people who don't do as well as we think we do. This is nonproductive.

Instead, our time alone with our Counselor should be used to allow Him to show us how we need to grow in being a channel for His love. He begins with how we are presently experiencing and expressing love. Decisively He helps us see our imperfections in loving.

∼

Often the Holy Spirit reveals to us that the very things about which we are most condemnatory may be hidden proclivities in ourselves.

∼

Each day, He amazes us anew with how much we are loved in spite of our failures and mistakes. Then He leads us through a review of our relationships. He projects on our mind's eye the faces of people at home, in our church, and at work. Since He knows those who have special needs for love at particular times, He brings them to our attention and helps us think through what we are to do and say.

The Holy Spirit presses us to see how we might have drifted into the presumptuous sin of condemnatory judgments that place people on the shelf as unworthy of our caring or active involvement. We need love from the Spirit to recommit ourselves to helping them deal with the things that upset us.

Often the Holy Spirit reveals to us that the very things about which we are most condemnatory may be hidden proclivities in ourselves. He also opens the closet of our own unforgiven memories that may make us severe judges of others. When we see people do things and we've been battling against the same temptation ourselves, we project onto them the punishment we'd mete out on ourselves if we put our tendency into action. Paul said, "Therefore you are inexcusable, O man, whoever you are who judge, for in whatever you judge another you condemn yourself; for you who judge do the same things" (Romans 2:1).

The Holy Spirit also is direct with us about how hard we become on people who have hurt us with their own judgments. He wants to free us from having multiplied the problem by evicting people from our lives because of the harm we think they've done to us.

GOOD ON YOU!

I have a Scottish friend who has a favorite blessing he announces to people. It's the old Scottish saying, "Gud on ye," meaning, "Good on you!" I wondered if he could say that to someone who had really hurt him. Then one day I saw him love a man who maliciously had tried to assassinate him with gossip. My friend communicated the ultimate good of unqualified love when, by human standards, the man who was trying to do him in could have been written off by him.

My friend is an excellent scholar, but also a counselee of the Holy Spirit. In his prayers about this malicious man, the Spirit had broken the destructive syndrome we all face. Hurt causes resentment, resentment schemes retaliation, and retaliation is expressed in punishment. When I asked my friend how the Holy Spirit broke this tendency in him, his response was very vivid.

"The Holy Spirit used the crowbar of the cross. On Calvary God broke the syndrome. Humankind deserved damnation; instead, God showered us with grace. Those of us who have received His grace through the cross now have the power not to carry resentment and refuse to retaliate. God didn't try to get even with us. Therefore, we are liberated from the need to get even with those who have hurt us."

Retaliation can be packaged in lots of different wrappings. It can be expressed in diffidence, neglect, a purgatorial pout that withholds affirmation. Or it can come with a blast of anger, or denigrating comments to others about the person to alter their estimate of him or her. Sometimes we try to block the person's future success just to balance accounts. We are the losers in the end. The boomerang is sent out, but it returns to hit and hurt our own souls. The shocking dynamic is that when we write off another person, we write off ourselves as people who, in our estimation, have a right to expect the love of God to be poured into our hearts by the Holy Spirit.

I'm thankful that the Holy Spirit doesn't give up on us, even when we do that. Goodness is also a fruit of His Spirit. He wants to make us people who can say, "Good on you!" to those we're tempted to write off in our thoughts, attitudes, or actions.

The Holy Spirit empowers us to pray the psalmist's deep desire, "Surely goodness and mercy shall follow me all the days of my life; and I will dwell in the house of the Lord forever" (Psalm 23:6). He does even better: He pours His goodness and mercy into our hearts. He knows how much we need both. We have an awesome calling to love others as Christ has loved us.

8 ∤ Overcoming Yesterday

WHAT'S THE MOST IMPORTANT thing you've learned about life?

If you wrote out a statement in twenty words or less beginning with "I have learned...," what would you say? What's the one thing you'd like to impart to your children, spouse, friends, or people with whom you work?

I was challenged to think about what I would want to express by a little book I read recently entitled *Live and Learn and Pass It On* by H. Jackson Brown.[1] He had an experience on his fifty-first birthday that moved him profoundly. The idea for the book rose out of that experience.

Brown took a sheet of paper and wrote, "I've learned that..." twenty times down the left side of the page. Then he spent the rest of the day completing the sentences. The experience was so stimulating that he repeats it every Sunday morning.

The thought hit him: why not begin collecting, "I've learned that..." statements from others? He made a special effort to include all ages of people from five to ninety-five from all over the nation. The responses he got were both inspiring and humorous. His book is a compilation of these "I've learned that..." statements.

I especially enjoyed the ones by children. I guess they appealed to the child in me. One seven-year-old wrote, "I've learned that you can't hide a piece of broccoli in a glass of milk." Another said, "I've learned that if you spread the peas out on your plate, it looks like you ate more." Then another made a difficult discovery, "I've learned that the tooth fairy doesn't always come. Sometimes he's broke." The imp in another was working overtime when he was at camp. "I've learned that if you want to get even with someone at camp, you rub their underwear in poison ivy." And still another said, "I've learned that my best friend is my teddy bear. He never tells my secrets."

~

"When you're on a fishing trip, the guy selling the bait always says, 'You should have been here yesterday!'"

~

The statements made by adults also were a rare blend of humor and insight. One eighty-four-year-old man wrote, "I've learned that the older I get, the more pretty girls I remember kissing as a young man." A middle-aged person had made a super discovery, "I've learned that even when I have pains, I don't have to be a pain." There's a prescription we all need to take and we all can think of a few people with whom we'd like to share this person's discovery.

"I've learned," wrote another man who is a duffer at golf, "that the quickest way to meet people is to pick up the wrong golf ball on the golf course."

Another said, "I've learned that there are four ages of a man: (1) when he believes in Santa Claus, (2) when he doesn't believe in Santa Claus, (3) when he is Santa Claus, and (4) when he looks like Santa Claus."

"I've learned that expensive new silk ties are the only ones that attract spaghetti sauce" one man groaned. And the fisherman in me empathized with the person who said, "I've learned that whenever I take a fishing trip, the guy who runs the bait shop always says, 'Gee, you should have been here yesterday.'"

After a good chuckle at these, I was moved by some of the more serious discoveries Brown had collected. Like these:

"I've learned that you can do something in an instant that will give you a heartache for life."

"I've learned that the great challenge of life is to decide what's important and to disregard everything else."

WHAT I HAVE LEARNED

I was so fascinated by Brown's experiment that I wrote to a number of people asking them to share with me what they've learned. I also started the practice of writing out some of the things I've learned. Some made me laugh, while others made me cry. I was painfully aware of how long it has taken me to learn some of the most important things I've discovered.

One of the most important things I learned under the guidance of the greatest Counselor in the world, the Holy Spirit, is something He has to reteach me repeatedly. If I'd been asked to submit the most significant thing I've learned for Brown's book, here is what it would be: "If you dote on yesterday's failures or successes, and worry about what might happen tomorrow, today will be a drag." Put another way, I've learned that I have to overcome my yesterdays, hold firm a magnificent obsession for my tomorrows, and live today as if it were the only day I had left.

WHAT PAUL LEARNED FROM THE HOLY SPIRIT

If we were to ask the apostle Paul what was the most important thing he'd learned from the greatest Counselor, I think he would say what he shared with his beloved friends in Philippi: "One thing I do, forgetting those things which are behind and reaching forward to those things which are ahead, I press forward to the goal for the prize of the upward call of God in Christ Jesus" (Philippians 3:13-14).

Here in one succinct thirty-six word affirmation is the secret the Holy Spirit gave Paul for overcoming his yesterdays. I'm glad the Holy Spirit inspired him to include his great discovery in his Philippians letter. It has been used by the Holy Spirit in the lives of Christian adventurers ever since. I have been drawn back to it countless times in my own counseling sessions with the Holy Spirit.

Whatever else you might say is the most important thing you've learned, something of the dynamic of Paul's statement needs to be included. If you're anything like me, you too find it difficult to sail into today with gusto if your anchor is stuck in the mud of yesterday.

So, in this chapter, let's do ourselves a favor and learn from the Holy Spirit what He taught Paul and wants to teach us. The best way I know to do that is to take Paul's statement phrase by phrase and allow the Holy Spirit to use whatever aspect of it he wants to reiterate for us to hear.

∼

Narrowing down our priorities to one basic motivating, liberating focus of our attention is a challenge. "Can you say 'One thing I do?'" the Holy Spirit asks.

∼

One thing. In many of the English versions of the Bible the word "do" in Paul's strong assertion, "One thing I *do*," is italicized. For good reason. There is no verb in the Greek text of this phrase. We could add *poieō* to the text giving it the verb "do," but it's not there in the original Greek manuscripts.

"One thing!" Paul exclaims. It's as if he's saying, "One thing, listen, one thing is really important to me and I hope to you." Narrowing down our priorities to one basic motivating, liberating focus of our attention is a challenge. "Can you say 'One thing I do?'" the Holy Spirit asks.

Many of us would have to say, "One thing? More like dozens or hundreds of things drive and call me in a multiplicity of directions." Even if we add the verb to Paul's phrase we'd have to say, "Many, many things I do and often feel I miss what I'm here to do." D.L. Moody said, "Give me a man who says, 'This one thing I do, and not these fifty things I dabble in.'"

It's fascinating to note that the Hebrew word for "dismayed" means to cast about furtively or look around with panic. The Lord's call to the Israelites was to keep their attention on Him. "Fear not, for I am with you; be not *dismayed,* for I am your God. I will strengthen you" (Isaiah 41:10). One thing. One assurance. One lasting source of courage. Who or what has our attention? The Holy Spirit wants to know.

Overcoming yesterday. Paul's "one thing" was his secret for overcoming his yesterdays. "Forgetting these things which are behind." What were the things from Paul's yesterdays that he was determined to forget? I think he meant both the bad things and the good things that had happened to him and through him.

For openers, Paul knew he had to forget the person he had been before his conversion. At no point in his epistles does he write of the delight of his student days training to be a Pharisee. There's no reference to his joy in the God of Israel prior to meeting Christ. None of the psalmist's exaltation. None of Jeremiah's compassion wrung out of mercies new every morning. No, the only memories were of vigilant, sterile legalism and fierce orthodoxy. A Hebrew of Hebrews, he called himself. According to the law, he was blameless. But he experienced no peace.

And then this from Paul's own pen. "Concerning zeal, persecuting the church." Yes, that could dominate Paul's memories of his yesterdays. He had stood by watching the mob stone Stephen; it could not have happened without a Pharisee's consent. Consent? He had instigated it. And he was more than ready to vent his rage on the followers of the crucified Nazarene when the Sanhedrin sent him to Damascus to round them up and incarcerate and punish them. He would never forget his encounter with Christ on the road. It was He, not just His followers, the Pharisee was persecuting! Paul had washed the blood off his hands; how did he ever wash out of his mind the memory of what he had done?

But there were some memories of other yesterdays after his conversion that he needed to forget. Could he ever forget the memory of that day on the first missionary journey when John Mark defected? Or was it that Paul lost his patience with the young man and sent him home? Little matter, there had been a failure in living out the message of reconciliation and forgiveness Paul preached so boldly. The apostle never quite got over that and near the end of his life did everything he could to reestablish his friendship with Mark. We can't help feeling that Paul called Timothy and treated him differently because of his sense of failure with Mark.

And what about Paul's open conflict with Peter? It's there for us to see in his first epistle, written to the Galatians. Paul felt he was right in his criticism of Peter, but did he ever regret not having put into practice his own clearly articulated procedures for conflict resolution?

Also think about the enemies Paul had to deal with all through his ministry. The Judaizers dogged his steps trying to disrupt the newborn gentile Christians with the false doctrine that they must first become Jews and the men must be circumcised. We know Paul was disturbed by these equivocators, but did he carry the memory of their indefatigable, demeaning opposition? And what about the angry hostility he had felt from the Jewish officialdom in Jerusalem and in the synagogue of every city where the apostle brought the Gospel? Add to that the ridicule of the Greek philosophers, the disdain of the Romans, and the negative prejudgment of political leaders. How did Paul take the battering of so many people against him? Didn't his yesterdays wear him down?

~

Paul would never forget his encounter with Christ on the road. It was Jesus, not just His followers, the Pharisee was persecuting! He had washed the blood off his hands; how did he ever wash out of his mind the memory of what he had done?

~

Be sure to add to Paul's yesterdays his physical infirmity, what he called his "thorn in the flesh." Whether it was eye trouble as some suggest, or malaria, as others postulate, makes little difference. The point is that he endured physical problems. He prayed for Christ to heal him. In response Christ told him, "My grace is sufficient for you, for my strength is made perfect in weakness." Instead of pouting through the rest of his life and ministry, Paul responded, "Therefore most gladly I will rather boast in my infirmities, that the power of Christ may rest upon me. Therefore I take pleasure in infirmities, in reproaches, in needs, in persecutions, in distresses, for Christ's sake. For when I am weak, then I am strong" (2 Corinthians 12:9b-10).

We've talked about the difficulties the apostle had in his yesterdays. On the success side of the ledger, Paul had more than enough that might have kept him smugly satisfied with what he had accomplished. He could have polished the trophies of his many triumphs: thousands won to Christ, churches established over most of the then-known world, and even personal spiritual victories like the incredible fortitude in weakness we reviewed above. The remarkable thing was that Paul was so free of false pride, so willing to point away from himself to what Christ had done.

~

"My grace is sufficient for you, for my strength is made perfect in weakness."

~

There's no other explanation than the consistent counseling ministry of the Holy Spirit in his life. It was the greatest Counselor who enabled him to experience daily forgetting of the things that were behind and pay complete attention to God's "now" leading.

THE HEALER OF MEMORIES

That same Holy Spirit is working in you and me. He is the healer of memories. He wants to help us forget "the things which are behind." In counseling sessions with Him, He helps us recall the memories that are ever present in our conscious minds and some that hurt so much that we have crammed them down into our subconscious where they lurk. There they become energy-suckers, specters of unidentified fears and panic.

Some years ago as part of my growing experience of the Holy Spirit, I discovered the power of the simple prayer, "Holy Spirit, help me to overcome my yesterdays. You know me through and through; nothing is hidden from You. Since I can't hide from You, help me not to hide from myself. Dredge up the hurting memories and help me to receive or give the forgiveness Christ died on Calvary to make possible. Lead me to the cross. I lay myself open to Your gracious but firm help in confronting and healing anything in any yesterday that is keeping me from living at full potential."

Lingering in silent prayer, hurting memories are brought into sharp focus. Sometimes the drama of what happened is played out before my mind's eye. All the old emotions are reexperienced. Then there is quiet. A time to let go—a time for healing.

> Who bears in mind misfortunes gone
>   will live in fear of more.
> The happy man whose heart is right
>   gives no such shadows power.
> He bears in mind no haunting past,
>   To vex his week on Monday
> He has no graves within his mind
>   To visit every Sunday.[2]

The same healing process I experience with hurting memories takes place with past accomplishments whenever they become haughty memories. For me, anytime a past achievement becomes a false security and keeps me from tackling new and greater challenges, I know I'm doting on the past. Whatever the Lord has done in the past is nothing in comparison with what He wants to do. This is true at any stage of our lives. There's always so much more to learn, always people who need the Savior's love, always a battle with social injustice to be waged. Nothing robs tomorrow more of what the Lord has planned than satisfaction with yesterday. And the Holy Spirit is the Author of the divine discontent that makes resting on the oars unpleasant.

Don't misunderstand. I'm not suggesting that the joy of being used by God is wrong. The question is: who gets the glory? Here again, thanksgiving and praise is the creative antidote to false pride. Our intellect, talents, and opportunities, coupled with any spiritual gifts, are all provisions of grace. The more we allow the Holy Spirit to remind us of that, the more He can entrust new challenges to us.

∿

Lead me to the cross. I lay myself open to Your gracious but firm help in confronting and healing anything in any yesterday that is keeping me from living at full potential.

∿

One time when I had rested far too long on a spiritual plateau, I asked the Holy Spirit to show me what was wrong. The night after my prayer, I had a dream. I was in a tiny constricted hut at the bottom of the Grand Canyon. All of a sudden a mighty wind began to blow. The roof was blown off my hut and then the walls were knocked out, falling flat on the floor of the canyon. I beheld the breathtaking grandeur all around me. A voice reverberated around the canyon, "Why sit in a hut when all this is available to behold?" When I woke up I knew the meaning of the dream: closed in on myself, I was missing the magnificence the Holy Spirit was trying to help me enjoy.

THE MAGNIFICENT OBSESSION

Forgetting the things behind is only half the miracle of overcoming our yesterdays. We need a magnificent obsession to draw us on to the future. Catch the expectation in Paul, "And reaching forward to the things which are ahead, I press toward the goal for the prize of the upward call of God in Christ Jesus" (Philippians 3:13b-14). This compelling vision was instigated and inspired by the Holy Spirit. His purpose is to keep us focused on Christ and the next phase of the race. His goal is our growth in Christ and the prize of maturity in Him.

Again, a deeper look at Paul's words heightens our appreciation for the magnificent obsession that drew him on. The words "reaching forward" depict a runner stretching forward, leaning toward the goal, "going flat out for it," as the Scots would say. The Greek word for "goal" is *skopos* from *skopēo*, "to look at" (from which our word telescope comes). It denotes a mark on which to fix the eye. The word "prize" is fascinating. It is *brabeion,* the award for finishing the race. The word is closely related to *brabeus,* an umpire, or the one who judges the race and awards the prize. Paul's goal for his "high calling" of running the race of discipleship is Christ. He is also the Judge who will award Paul the crown (2 Timothy 4:1, 8). And the "upward call" into heaven would be the ultimate fulfillment of the eternal life he began in a house on a street called Straight in Damascus years before. Ananias had laid his hands on him saying, "Brother Saul, the Lord Jesus, who appeared to you on the road as you came has sent me that you may receive your sight and be filled with the Holy Spirit" (Acts 9:17). From then on Paul's life was magnificently focused on Christ and mightily empowered by the Holy Spirit. He was sure of the upward call to heaven all through his life on earth.

ALL THIS AND HEAVEN TOO

To use a very different twist on a title of an old movie, the Christian life is, "All this and heaven too." During this portion of our eternal life, we are meant to enjoy the race knowing that we're going to win. Abundant life in Christ is inseparable from the goal of eternal life. C.S. Lewis was right, "Aim at heaven and you get earth thrown in. Aim at earth and you will get neither."[3]

One of the people who responded to my collection of the greatest things they had learned is a man who lately has been the fast-moving target of the Holy Spirit. He wrote the following note:

You've asked about the greatest thing I learned: let me tell you what I've had to *un*learn. For years I've been racing on the fast track toward my goals of success and material security. It's been a rat race, and by all outward signs I was way out front. At forty-nine, I had reached all my goals but was not satisfied. I don't know who said it but it's true: "Life becomes intolerable only to those who feel there's nothing more for which they can live and nothing to which they can aspire."

I hear you talk a lot about abundant and eternal life. I know you're not talking about material abundance but spiritual blessings like peace and joy, both of which I haven't had. As far as eternal life, you say it begins now and death can't end it. I've had to honestly admit that my conscious goals have not included heaven. Recently, I've really been uncomfortable, disquieted inside. This has led me to spend time each day with the Holy Spirit, as you suggested. Following your lead, I've laid out my life before him. The question He's asked me is, "If you arrive at where you've been heading with such intensity, where will you be?" It's been dawning on me that even though I'm a nominal Christian, I have not had the experience of the abundant life or an assurance of eternal life. I've pitched my goals too low.

One day alone in my prayer I made a new commitment to Christ as my Savior and Lord and asked to be filled with the Holy Spirit. The result has been a profound *unlearning* process. I've felt the presence of God in my life as never before. Every day I start out with a fresh commitment to spend that day intentionally serving Christ. The Holy Spirit keeps a consistent conversation going inside me about how best to do that. I've got to tell you that I'm unlearning my old values and goals and learning new ones. And the peace and joy have begun to flow, even in the toughest times.

The most difficult thing to unlearn is that the money I

earn isn't my own. This crusty old materialist is finally discovering the joy of giving it away to people and programs that will count for Christ.

This is all more than the twenty words or less you asked for, but I thought I'd use this opportunity to check in and tell you what's been happening in my life.

ACCOUNTABILITY TIME

Now it's accountability time for you and me. Can we really say that Christ is the impelling passion and purpose for us? Is He the goal of the race we're running? Our Counselor keeps asking those crucial questions. The words "staying on track" mean staying on track as you run the race. Imagine a runner leaving the track and running all over the stadium. It would look absurd, wouldn't it? That's what happens when we forget that we are in a race, heading toward a goal. The Holy Spirit constantly calls us back into the race. He exposes the lesser goals that we think are the real prize: power, money, possessions, success for our glory, people, and human accolades.

Our problem is that we try to run two races at the same time: one for the goal of what our culture conditions us to think is important; the other is toward the goal of Christ. The Holy Spirit helps us to run *one* race to glorify Christ. Everything else we do has meaning and purpose only if we do it for Christ's glory. Then our relationships, work, and activities begin to take on new meaning. They are part of the race and demand our very best. All of life becomes a unified whole instead of a fractured source of stress.

The Holy Spirit's strategy for helping us overcome our yesterdays is not only to heal our hurting memories and loosen our dependence on past accomplishments, but also to press us on to the next phase of the race. It's one of the most crucial things Paul learned from the Holy Spirit. We're thankful. The words the apostle wrote under the inspiration of the Holy Spirit describing what he'd learned about forgetting yesterday and pressing on to tomorrow have become a motto for Christians ever since. From the application of Paul's words to my life, the Holy Spirit has taught me the most important thing I've learned. It has led me to adapt a poem by Benton Braley:

Run on from where you stand and never mind the past
The past can't help you when you're beginning new
If you have left it all behind at last
Then you're done with it, you're through.
This is a new chapter in the book
Today is a new lap in the race He's planned.
Don't give the vanished days a backward look
Run on from where you stand.

Old failures need not halt, old triumphs never aid
Today's the thing, tomorrow soon will be;
Get in the race and run it unafraid
And leave the past to ancient history;
What has been is forgiven; yesterday is dead,
And by it you are neither blessed or banned.
Take courage then, be brave and press ahead
Run on from where you stand![4]

9 | Ready for Battle: Discerning and Armed

W E ARE AT WAR. You and I are involved in a deadly, daily battle with a formidable foe. His name is Satan.

The greatest Counselor in the world, the Holy Spirit, is with us to help us be overcomers. His assignment is to be sure we claim Christ's encouragement: "In this world you will have tribulation; but be of good cheer, I have overcome the world" (John 16:33); and the apostle John's assurance, "You have overcome the wicked one" (1 John 2:14). The Spirit equips us for battle and is the strategist for daily victory. To prepare us to receive His help we need to do some realistic thinking about spiritual warfare. Here are some biblical presuppositions to keep our thinking straight.

Presupposition one: There is in the world an objective force of evil, marshalling his forces against the people of God.

Presupposition two: Those who believe in Jesus Christ and have trusted Him as Lord and Savior are the special target of the forces of evil. Satan's techniques are to try to discourage, dissemble, confuse, put down, insinuate, and hurt. His ultimate goal is to make us question that we belong to Christ and to try to take from us the assurance of our faith.

~

The greatest Counselor in the world is our Armorbearer, Who equips us with the whole armor of God for the battle with Satan.

~

Presupposition three: Jesus Christ came into the world to defeat the power of evil and Satan. He went to the cross and when He died on the cross, as His blood was shed, victory was won. Now, in the interface between Pentecost and Christ's second coming, we live in the midst of a world influenced by Satan's power. However, you and I have a Name that is greater than the name of the force of evil and that is the Name of Jesus Christ. Through Him, you and I are overcomers.

Presupposition four: The greatest Counselor in the world is our Armorbearer, Who equips us with the whole armor of God for the battle with Satan. One of the uses of the word *Paraklētos* was for one who stood by as an armorbearer in battle. Our daily times of counseling with the Holy Spirit, particularly each morning, are times in the armory in which He wants to suit us up for the battle. He did it for Paul and inspired the apostle to write to the Ephesians about various weapons God has designed for our warfare with the evil one. What the Holy Spirit inspired Paul to write is now used by Him to help us identify our armor and be overcomers in battles with Satan.

Finally, my brethren, be strong in the Lord and in the power of his might. Put on the whole armor of God, that you may be able to stand against the wiles of the devil. For we do not wrestle against flesh and blood, but against principalities, against powers, against the rulers of the darkness of this age, against spiritual wickedness in the heavenly places. Therefore take up the whole armor of God, that you may be able to withstand in the evil day, and having done all, to stand. Stand therefore, having girded your waist with truth, having put on the breastplate of righteousness, and having shod your feet with the preparation of the Gospel of peace; above all, taking the shield of faith with which you will be able to quench all the fiery darts of the wicked one. And take the helmet of salvation, and the sword of the Spirit, which is the word of God. **Ephesians 6:10-17**

Paul's challenge, "Finally, brethren, be strong in the Lord," (Ephesians 6:10) in the Greek really means, "Let the Lord make you strong." The present passive imperative indicates that He makes us strong in union with Him through the Holy Spirit. Then, with a marvelous kind of thrust, with the aorist imperative, Paul says "Put on the whole armor of God." It's as if he's crying out to the Ephesians, "Put it on! Put it on now! Put it on definitely! Put it on every day! Put on the whole armor of God!" Why? That we may be able to withstand the wiles of the devil. The word "wiles" means Satan's clever scheming. Someone once said the favorite wiles of the devil are "wait a while." But his wiles are much more conniving and manipulative than that.

THE GIFT OF DISCERNMENT

This is why the Holy Spirit, our Counselor, seeks to equip us with one of His most important gifts. This gift is listed among the nine primary gifts of the Spirit in 1 Corinthians, chapter twelve. It is the gift of discerning the spirits (1 Corinthians 12:10). When we face difficult times, it is absolutely essential to discern whether the cause has been our own mistakes or unwillingness to follow guidance; the mischief of other people motivated by selfishness, envy, or competitiveness; the work of Satan; or something the Lord has allowed to help us grow.

~

When life goes bump and problems mount, the first question to ask in our counseling session with the Holy Spirit is, "What, if anything, did I do or say to cause this mess I'm in?"

~

In our counseling sessions with the Holy Spirit, we can talk through what's happening to and around us. Then in quiet listening to Him, He gives this supernatural gift of discernment. The Greek word for discernment is *diakrisis*, signifying to separate, discriminate, to determine and decide. The gift of discernment enables us to detect the power of evil at work in a situation, person, or group. It helps us to determine whether something is part of Satan's diabolical influence, his outright destructive plan, or whether it is something the Spirit is trying to teach us. This is a crucial gift when so many beguiling people, ideas, and causes parade themselves as authentic when they may, in fact, be Satan's tools, his wiles, his scheming.

When life goes bump and problems mount, the first question to ask in our counseling session with the Holy Spirit is, "What, if anything, did I do or say to cause this mess I'm in?" Total honesty and openness to whatever the Holy Spirit helps us discern was our own fault, prepares us for confession and assurance of forgiveness. The reason this is so important is that sometimes we try to camouflage our own willfulness as a wile of Satan. When we are open to the possibility that we may be the cause, the slate is wiped clean before Satan can try to influence us with remorseful self-incrimination. He can't do that when, on an hourly and daily basis, we lay ourselves open to the Holy Spirit to help us own our mistakes and then disown them through forgiveness.

When our difficulties seem to be caused by people or groups, we need the Holy Spirit's discernment to evaluate whether their words or actions are, indeed, a message from the Lord or are caused by their own needs. Something we've done may have caused their reaction, or they may be motivated by an evil intent to destroy and may even be manipulated by Satan. Again, when we talk through with the Holy Spirit what's happening, He will help us determine the real cause.

~

People can be pawns of Satan on the chessboard of life to threaten us, fill us with panic, or cause us to question our worth.

~

After we have done all we can to correct a situation, seek reconciliation, and explain ourselves, if someone persists in a destructive way, the Holy Spirit may give us discernment that we are battling not just with human reactions but evil intent. People can be pawns of Satan on the chessboard of life to threaten us, fill us with panic, or cause us to question our worth. The reverse is also a dangerous possibility. Without the consistent counseling of the Holy Spirit, we too can drift into a place where we can be influenced by Satan to be destructive toward other people. We need a constant check to be sure whether what we are doing or saying is motivated by envy, greed, the desire to dominate—or the desire to love creatively by the Spirit's power and grace.

We also need the Holy Spirit to give us discernment when we are undergoing rigorous training by the Lord to toughen the fiber of our discipleship. Years ago in a time of pressure and tension, my good friend, Dr. Robert Munger, distinguished pastor and professor and my covenant brother in a prayer group, gave me a poem that I've cherished. I've never been able to find the name of the poet who penned it, but recently I found it in a book of illustrative material by Michael P. Green. Reading it again brought back the same impact it had on me years ago.

The poem originally spoke about a man. I've changed that to "person" because it applies to both men and women.

> When God wants to drill a person
> And thrill a person
> When God wants to mold a person
> To play the noblest part
>
> When He yearns with all His heart
> To create so great and bold a person
> That all the world shall be amazed
> Watch His methods, watch His ways—
> How He ruthlessly perfects
> Whom He royally elects
>
> How He bends but never breaks
> When His good He undertakes
> How He uses whom He chooses
> And with every purpose, fuses
> By every act, induces
> To try His splendor out
> God knows what He's about.[1]

It is the Holy Spirit's assignment to help us discern when the Lord is allowing us to go through learning experiences that will help us grow spiritually. He prompts us to ask, "What can I get out of this?" rather than moaning, "Just get me out of this!" Most important, the Holy Spirit enables us to know when what's happening is from the Lord or from Satan. Satan's strategy is to try to cripple us spiritually and put us out of commission. His scheming includes temptations to compromise what we believe or to behave in ways that contradict our moral integrity. Let's face it. He wants us to fail, to make willful mistakes, and to try to run our own lives. When we fail, he engulfs us in self-blame and shame for what we have said or done. The Holy Spirit seeks to warn and alert us to these wiles by equipping us with discernment. He is both our Discerner and Armorbearer.

~

It is the Holy Spirit's assignment to help us discern when the Lord is allowing us to go through learning experiences that will help us grow spiritually.

~

Notice in the passage quoted earlier from Ephesians how the apostle Paul marches before us the gathered army of Satan, his demons, and all his forces of evil. He uses different terms, but all of them mean that there is in this world the force of evil seeking to undermine the work of Christ, unsettle Christians, make us anxious, and rob us of our security. In the midst of the danger, the apostle Paul then says: Put on this *whole* armor. He proceeds to describe it part by part in a wonderful way. The Holy Spirit hands each piece of armament to us and helps us put it on when we spend time with Him as our Counselor.

THE BELT OF TRUTH

First of all we are to gird around our waists the belt of truth. The lumbar region of our backs is equipped to help us to stand up straight. The belt of truth gives us strong backs spiritually. It helps us to know who we are and to Whom we belong. That is the source of our courage in the midst of the battle.

Remember that the Holy Spirit is the Spirit of truth (John 14:17). The admonition to put on the belt of truth is another way of saying, "Be filled with the Spirit" (Ephesians 5:18).

I like to string together some of the verses from 1 John in claiming our role as overcomers. Put on the belt as I paraphrase some verses from 1 John 2:13, 4:4, 5:4, and 5:18. Claim that you *have* overcome the evil one. "You are of God and therefore, the One who is in you, the Holy Spirit, is greater than the one who is in the world. And you who believe that Jesus Christ is the Son of God can overcome the world. You are born of God and are an overcomer."

Put that belt of truth around the lumbar region of your soul, so that the Holy Spirit can give you support and strength. In the midst of Satan's untruth, dissimulation, and conniving plans to confuse, we can stand on the truth.

~

Jesus said, "You shall know the truth, and the truth shall make you free" (John 8:32). This truth is the ultimate, absolute reality about God, about life, about the means of salvation in and through Christ's death that set us free.

~

Christ is the truth. "I am the way, the truth, and the life" (John 14:6). There is no ultimate truth apart from Him. And in His truth, all other truth falls into its rightful place. It is the responsibility of the Holy Spirit to make us sure of this truth.

Jesus said, "You shall know the truth, and the truth shall make you free" (John 8:32). This truth is the ultimate, absolute reality about God, about life, about the means of salvation in and through Christ's death that set us free. We know that we belong to Him and that will never change.

We know something else. There is a truth that gives us special strength for the battle: when we belong to Jesus Christ we are surrounded by a protective seal. Satan can try to influence our minds and attack our emotions, but he cannot possess us.

We have been sealed with the Holy Spirit. Remember, "You were sealed with the Holy Spirit of promise, who is the guarantee of our inheritance, until the redemption of the purchased possession, to the praise of his glory" (Ephesians 1:13-14).

~

There is a truth that gives us special strength for the battle: when we belong to Jesus Christ we are surrounded by a protective seal.

~

If there is anyone reading this who does not know Jesus Christ as Lord and Savior, who has never turned his or her life over to Him, who has never been filled with the Holy Spirit, you're living in a perilous state. You can be attacked or possessed and can even become a tool of Satan in the midst of the world. Claim Jesus' Name. Give your life to Him. Don't wait. Do it now. And let Him fill you with the Holy Spirit so that you can know the truth.

We are living in a time of history when so many are troubled about confusing ideologies and New Age philosophies. We are to take our stand in the midst of the confusion, saying there's no new age apart from Christ as Lord and Savior. There is no intimate knowledge of God in any occult practice or belief. There is no hope in any kind of scientific materialism or humanism. Only in Jesus Christ can we stand. That's the truth. Let the Holy Spirit gird you with that truth.

BREASTPLATE OF RIGHTEOUSNESS

Next, the Holy Spirit helps us put on the breastplate of righteousness. Some biblical interpreters have asserted that the breastplate was just for the front and not for the back. They have admonished, "Face the enemy head-on. Don't ever turn your back on him." However, careful study reveals that a Roman soldier's breastplate covered both his front and his back and went from his neck down to his hips. Some were made of metal petals that were woven together; others were hammered out of metal so that they fit perfectly on the chest and the back of the soldier. So on either side or even when turning for a moment, he was always protected from the enemy. What a marvelous image!

But why is righteousness a breastplate? When we know the righteousness of God and have accepted that we are right with Him, by faith, and that we are justified by Him, a security grows deep inside of us. We know that for now and for eternity we belong to the Lord. The apostle Paul said: "[I have a] righteousness which is through faith in Christ, the righteousness which is from God by faith" (Philippians 3:9).

∼

Often we are defeated on the battlefield of daily conflict because we have not allowed the Holy Spirit to reestablish in our hearts an unassailable security in our standing as a loved, forgiven, and cherished son or daughter of the Father.

∼

We need this security every day. Satan tries to use people and problems to make us insecure in our relationship with the Father. He would like to use what happens in life to make us doubt our status with the Father. In our counseling sessions of prayer with the Holy Spirit, He helps us do battle with these doubts before we do battle in the struggles of life. Often we are defeated on the battlefield of daily conflict because we have not allowed the Holy Spirit to reestablish in our hearts an unassailable security in our standing as a loved, forgiven, and cherished son or daughter of the Father.

The breastplate of righteousness must be put on daily because it covers the area where we *feel* the security of a right relationship with the Father or suffer from a lack of it. Would you agree that you feel things in your chest? I do. When my thinking about something causes anxiety, I feel the anguish in my torso.

Let me illustrate with a common need we all have. We want to be liked and approved by other people. Nothing wrong in that except when we experience the withdrawal of some people's affirmation and acceptance, we can become vulnerable emotionally. Satan's attack can come through several persons' criticisms or harsh judgments falling on us all at once.

~

In prayer, I spread out the hurting words before Him.
He helped me reclaim my self-esteem as a person
who is valued by my Heavenly Father.

~

A leader is especially vulnerable to this kind of attack on his or her security. I had one such attack recently. Even though I have enjoyed more than my share of popularity and know that I can't please all the people all the time, one day I needed to retreat into a profound time of fellowship with the Holy Spirit to get the breastplate of righteousness back on and in place. On that day I received a blast of criticism from several people. A man criticized my preaching, another raised a question about my management style, still another blamed me for having to wait a few days for an appointment. And so it went all through the day. One disgruntled person after another.

By afternoon I knew that I had to get time alone with my Counselor before I responded to any of these people. In prayer, I spread out the hurting words before Him. He helped me reclaim my self-esteem as a person who is valued by my Heavenly Father. The Holy Spirit seemed to be saying, "Your task is not to please people but to serve them. If there is any truth in what has been said, face it, and I will give you strength and courage to change what needs to be changed. And where you are being criticized for the wrong reasons, I will give you confidence to press on seeking the kingdom of God and His righteousness." The change in the feeling in my chest was remarkable. I experienced a profound sense of security in God's love and acceptance of me through the practical, on the spot counseling of the Holy Spirit.

Leaders of all kinds tell me they have days, sometimes weeks, when pressure from negative people builds up. Business people tell me about days when customers and employees and loved ones all fire their guns at once on what seems to be a day of open hunting for accumulated wrongs. One man I know vividly calls those days a "demonic gang-rape" on his security in Christ. A mother and housewife said, "I've had one of those days! My daughter, husband, a neighbor, and a good friend decided independently that this was the day to straighten me out. I could take any one of them, but it's the impact of it all in one day. I feel shattered!"

~

The righteousness of God enables us to live in the midst of the battles of life knowing that we are secure.

~

We can't make it through days like that, or any day for that matter, without the help of the Holy Spirit. This is why I've had to learn to take my quiet time with the Holy Spirit, my Counselor, first thing, even before I shower and dress for the day. And then at the end of the day, I find it absolutely essential to reevaluate what's happened in the day with the Holy Spirit's gift of discernment. Without that I'd be a target for discouragement that would rob me of my security in Christ and my joy of knowing that, in spite of everything, I am cherished and valued. With that I can sleep soundly and the next day correct what's wrong and stick by what's right.

The righteousness of God enables us to live in the midst of the battles of life knowing that we are secure. Let the Spirit help you don the breastplate of righteousness, so you can experience that kind of security today and every day of your life.

SHOES OF PEACE

But there's more. Next, the Holy Spirit encourages us to shoe our feet with the preparation of the Gospel of peace (Ephesians 6:15). He wants us to learn what He taught Paul. The apostle observed the shoes on Roman soldiers. They were half-boots called *caliga*, made of leather, open at the toes and tied around the ankles and shins with straps. The soles were thick and heavy, studded with lognails. This gave a soldier sure-footed stability to take a stand in battle. The thickness of the soles also protected the Roman soldier from one of the most clever devices of an enemy. Often in the field where the Roman soldiers met an enemy for battle, there would be short, sharp spears protruding from the ground, hidden in among the grass so that the soldiers couldn't see them. As the soldiers marched on, their feet would be pierced unless they had thick soled shoes. I believe that this is some of what Paul had in mind when he described shoeing our feet with the preparation of the Gospel of peace.

~

Our Counselor wants us to be sure of our peace.
A fruit of His indwelling is true peace.

~

The Holy Spirit helps us understand this metaphor He first impressed on the apostle's mind. Our Counselor wants us to be sure of our peace. A fruit of His indwelling is true peace. He reminds us of Jesus' assurance, "Peace I leave with you, my peace I give to you; not as the world gives do I give to you. Let not your heart be troubled, neither let it be afraid" (John 14:27). The daily ministry of the Holy Spirit is to renew our experience of authentic peace. He did it for Paul and gave him the clarity to declare the source and substance of peace. "Therefore, having been justified by faith, we have peace with God through our Lord Jesus Christ" (Romans 5:1). Lasting peace is the result of knowing that we are loved and forgiven.

In his second letter to the Thessalonians, Paul wrote a benediction that underlines the amazing staying power of real peace. "Now may the Lord of peace Himself give you peace always in every way. The Lord be with you all" (2 Thessalonians 3:16). Always and in every way? That's quite a promise. The presence of the Lord in the power of the Holy Spirit makes this possible.

~

The peace the Holy Spirit enables is the result of a forgiven and a forgiving heart.

~

The Greek word for peace is *eirēnē*. And the Hebrew word is *shaloam*. When Paul used the word peace he meant total well-being, harmony between us and God, and reconciliation and good will between us and others. An aspect of *eirēnē* means the knitting together of what's ravelled and torn. The Holy Spirit is the divine repairer of the fabric of our hearts. Again, He gives us the discernment to detect what has torn or frayed our ongoing experience of peace. ✔

The peace the Holy Spirit enables is the result of a forgiven and a forgiving heart. There can be no real peace if there is anything unconfessed or anything we need to forgive that

someone has done to us. We can seek forgiveness, forgive ourselves, and communicate forgiveness only if we have a steady
flow of grace, knowing we are loved. So, peace is also the
result of a love-captivated heart. Then, too, peace resides in a
surrendered heart, ready and willing to do God's will. Henry
Van Dyke expressed his own process of experiencing peace
through relinquishment of his will to the Lord:

> With eager heart and will on fire
> I sought to win my heart's desire
> "Peace will be mine," I said. But life
> grew bitter in the endless strife.
>
> My soul was weary, and my pride
> was wounded deep. To heaven I cried
> "God give me peace, or I must die."
> The dumb stars glittered not reply.
>
> Broken at last I bowed my head
> forgetting all myself and said:
> "Whatever comes, His will be done"
> and in that moment peace was won.[2]

Day by day, the Holy Spirit helps us confront anything that
would rob us of profound inner peace. He enables us to ask
for and receive forgiveness for our failures and mistakes. He
knows how crucial this is in our spiritual warfare with Satan,
who is always ready to incriminate us and makes us insecure.
The Holy Spirit reaffirms in us what He revealed to Paul,
"The peace of God, which surpasses all understanding, will
guard your hearts and minds through Christ Jesus" (Philippians 4:7, emphasis mine).

Now we can understand why Paul used the word "preparation" in describing the Gospel of peace. The Greek word *het-oimasia* means readiness or surefooted foundation. This is the unassailable peace the Holy Spirit renews in us each day, which makes us surefooted in the slippery places of our combat with Satan.

~

The Holy Spirit reaffirms in us what He revealed to Paul, "The peace of God, which surpasses all understanding, will guard your hearts and minds through Christ Jesus."

~

The Gospel of peace also recruits us as peacemakers who are on the offensive in the conflicts and misunderstandings around us. The best defense against Satan is an offense. We are on the alert to act with alacrity in expressing whatever will bring peace in our relationships. The Holy Spirit guides us in what to say and do. He knows how perilous it is to allow anything to fester, giving Satan an opportunity to do his mischief.

One morning recently, as the Holy Spirit was equipping me with the whole armor and I was mentally putting on the shoes of peace, He reminded me of a resentment I had carried over several days. It was keeping me from feeling at peace. A friend had hurt me deeply. Foolishly, I had nursed the resentment. That morning I asked the Holy Spirit to counsel me on what to do. In the quiet, as I put on the shoes of peace, He showed me that I had to surrender my resentment and forgive the man. "Do it now," the Spirit seemed to say, "and then go to him today and tell him you have forgiven him." I followed the Spirit's orders and peace flooded my heart again.

Further, the shoes for preparation of the Gospel of peace give us quick and cheerful readiness to be communicators of peace to those around us who do not know Christ. We think of Isaiah 52:7, "How beautiful upon the mountains are the feet of him who brings good news, who proclaims peace."

Christ fulfilled this messianic image, and we who belong to Him are proclaimers of His peace. One of the most effective ways of sharing our faith is to be open with people about what Christ's peace has done for us in the stresses of daily life. People are drawn to those who radiate true peace. In the context of a caring relationship with them, often they will want to know the reason for our serenity when facing life's pressures. The Holy Spirit keeps us alert for opportunities to share what the love and forgiveness of Christ can do to give them lasting peace. We can explain the release from tension that comes through the surrender of our lives and problems to the Lord and the resiliency that results from being filled daily with the Holy Spirit.

∼

The Gospel of peace also recruits us as peacemakers who are on the offensive in the conflicts and misunderstandings around us.

∼

Of course, Satan abhors this spreading of the Gospel. He tries to impede us with reserve or timidity. But daily renewal of our experience of peace makes us all the more determined to share with others the secret of lasting peace which the Holy Spirit has given us. Satan would like us to buy into the idea that whatever we do, it won't make any difference. That's why we need the next part of our armor.

SHIELD OF FAITH

We can't survive in spiritual warfare without the shield of faith. A Roman soldier's shield was made up of wood and linen braced with iron and covered with pitch, so he could hold it up and resist the fiery darts of the enemy.

We need a shield that can withstand the fiery darts of the devil. These darts are doubt, discouragement, and mistrust. The only protection is the shield of faith. The Holy Spirit gives us a fresh supply of vital, applicable faith each day. He knows how much we need it. We are surrounded by people who are more convinced about what God can't do than what He can and will do.

∽

Self-reliance leaves our hearts unprotected when crises hit. The Holy Spirit wants to give us the courage to ask, "What does the Lord want?"

∽

I was in a meeting recently in which all the solutions offered to problems were within the limits of what we could do on our own inadequate strength. The fiery darts of doubt were flying, setting fires of fear in people's hearts. I kept holding up the invisible shield of faith to resist Satan's attack through the panic people were expressing.

This happened during a budget meeting of a board of a Christian organization on which I serve. We had not spent as much time praying about how to plan wisely and courageously as we had spent in discussing the budget. I was greatly relieved when the chairman of the board called for a prolonged period of prayer. After asking for the Holy Spirit to guide us, we sat in silent prayer. When we resumed our discussion, there was a new spirit of faith as we reevaluated the goals of the organization and drafted the final budget in keeping with what we all could agree the Lord would provide. At the end of the fiscal year, the exact amount had been provided through the faithful donors to this organization.

Self-reliance leaves our hearts unprotected when crises hit. The Holy Spirit wants to give us the courage to ask, "What does the Lord want?" Then He provides the faith to trust that what He guides us to pray for will be done. Each morning in the armory, He hands us the shield of faith saying, "Today, don't base your expectations on what you assume God can't do! Ask for and receive the gift of faith to pray with boldness."

But what goes on inside of our hearts is controlled by what's in our heads. That's why the Holy Spirit helps us put on the helmet of salvation. In 1 Thessalonians 5:8, Paul calls it the helmet of the hope of salvation.

HELMET OF SALVATION

The helmet of a Roman soldier protected his head. The implication is that the helmet of salvation protects our thinking. It keeps Satan from invading our thoughts with distorted ideas, plans that will lead us away from our ultimate goal, and muddled thinking that will immobilize our discipleship. All through our lives we need to think straight about salvation. We have been saved. We did not deserve it nor must we earn it. We are being saved. Each day the Holy Spirit leads us further into the grand assurance that we belong to God. The Holy Spirit helps us become whole people, healed and released. And He keeps reminding us that we are on the way to heaven. No wonder He insists that we put on the helmet of salvation!

~

As we put on the helmet of salvation, we are given Christ-esteem from which healthy self-esteem really comes.

~

Each morning in our counseling session with the Holy Spirit He helps us regain that precious gift of self-esteem we've talked about. As we put on the helmet of salvation, we are given Christ-esteem from which healthy self-esteem really comes. Through Christ we experience the essence of creative self-esteem: we gain the confidence of our personal worth. The Holy Spirit's ministry is to convince us of our worth every day, reminding us that we are loved, forgiven, and cherished. He helps us to picture a scale. On one side are placed all the things we have done or been that we hold against ourselves. On the other side the Spirit places the cross and the unlimited grace given to us. Then each day we see in our mind's eye how the cross not only balances the scale but tips it over on the side of grace.

To put on the helmet of salvation each day is a radical act. Yes, radical. The word "radical" means to the roots. Every day we need a radical reorientation of our thinking about ourselves. The love and forgiveness of the cross must reach down into the roots of our self-condemnatory, self-depreciating, self-justifying thinking. The Holy Spirit is ready to help us if we will ask Him, "Holy Spirit, heal my distorted thinking about myself today. Penetrate to the very roots of my thoughts and give me Christ-esteem."

One way I can be sure I have prayed this prayer and claimed the healing results is to respond to the question "How are you?" by saying, "I am blessed!" This helps me reaffirm often throughout the day that I have the helmet of salvation on. I have been saved, I'm being saved, and I will be saved. Or put another way: I have been loved, I am being loved, and I will be loved in whatever happens.

SWORD OF THE WORD

Once the Holy Spirit has helped us secure our helmet, we are ready to wield the "sword of the Spirit which is the word of God" (Ephesians 6:17). The sword referred to here is a short dirk that was used by a Roman soldier in hand-to-hand combat. The Holy Spirit wants to equip us with His sword because our confrontation with Satan is often one-on-one. In many situations and problems of life, we need a sword for hands-on combat with Satan.

In *Pilgrim's Progress,* John Bunyan vividly portrays Christian's sword battle with Apollyon, the angel of death, in the Valley of Humiliation. The combat lasted half a day and Christian grew weary and weak. While wrestling with Apollyon, he fell and his sword flew from his hand. Apollyon thought he had his victim now. But just as he prepared to strike his final blow, Christian reached out and grasped his sword. He thrust it through the angel of death saying, "Rejoice not against me, O mine enemy; when I fall I shall arise." With that he gave Apollyon a mortal wound, and he spread forth his broken wings and sped away. "In these things we are more than conquerors through Him who loved us," Christian said triumphantly.

In real life, the sword is no less effective in our combat with Satan. But what exactly is this powerful weapon?

∾

The Holy Spirit inspired the writing of the Bible, so He knows exactly what word, verse, or passage will help us when Satan attacks.

∾

The sword of the Spirit is the Word of God (Ephesians 6:17). In the Greek, *rhēma* is used for "word" rather than *logos.* Christ is the eternal Logos, the ultimate Word of God. The word *rhēma* means "a particular saying." For example, we have the sayings of God in the Old Testament and the words of Christ that have been preserved for us in the Gospels. The Holy Spirit inspired the writing of the Bible, so He knows exactly what word, verse, or passage will help us when Satan attacks. In each trying situation, He hands us a sharp sword that will be able to stab Satan and send him limping away. The Bible is an armory filled with these swords or dirks. The Holy Spirit selects the one that's just right for the situation.

Here are some of the *rhēma* dirks the Holy Spirit has given me in times of need:

- "I will call upon the Lord, who is worthy to be praised; so shall I be delivered from my enemies" (2 Samuel 22:4).

- "God is our refuge and strength, a very present help in trouble. Therefore we will not fear" (Psalm 46:1-2b).

- "The Lord rebuke you, Satan!" (Zechariah 3:2).

- "Away with you, Satan!" (Matthew 4:10).

- "Be sober, be vigilant; because your adversary the devil walks about like a roaring lion, seeking whom he may devour. Resist him, steadfast in the faith, knowing that the same sufferings are experienced by your brotherhood in the world" (1 Peter 5:8-9).

- "No temptation has overtaken you except such as is common to man; but God is faithful, who will not allow you to be tempted beyond what you are able, but with the temptation will also make the way of escape, that you may be able to bear it" (1 Corinthians 10:13).

- "He is able to aid those who are tempted" (Hebrews 2:18).

- "He is able to keep you from stumbling" (Jude 24).

- "He is also able to save to the uttermost" (Hebrews 7:25).

- "For the weapons of our warfare are not carnal but mighty through God for pulling down strongholds, casting down arguments and every high thing that exalts itself against the knowledge of God, bringing every thought into captivity to the obedience of Christ..." (2 Corinthians 10:4-6).

- "He who is in you is greater than he who is in the world" (1 John 4:4).

For example, when I am exhausted and need strength, and Satan tries to sell me on the idea that if I just try harder and work longer I'll make it, the Spirit uses a *rhēma* like Isaiah 40:31, "But those who wait on the Lord shall renew their strength; they shall mount up with wings like eagles, they shall run and not be weary, they shall walk and not faint."

Or, when Satan plays on my fears, Isaiah 43:1-2 becomes a sword of the Spirit: "Fear not, for I have redeemed you; I have called you by your name; you are Mine. When you pass through the waters, I will be with you; and through the rivers, they shall not overflow you."

I wield Jeremiah 33:3 as a sword when I feel boxed in on all sides by what Satan parades as impossibilities. These are the Lord's words: "Call to Me, and I will answer you, and show you great and mighty things, which you do not know."

∽

"Fear not, for I have redeemed you, I have called you by your name; you are Mine. When you pass through the waters, I will be with you; and through the rivers, they shall not overflow you." Isaiah 43:1-2

∽

When Satan tries to muddle my thinking and I need to be sure my priorities are straight, Jeremiah 9:23-24 becomes a sword of the Spirit. "Let not the wise man glory in his wisdom, let not the mighty man glory in his might, nor let the rich man glory in his riches; but let him who glories glory in this, that he understands and knows Me, that I am the Lord, exercising lovingkindness, judgment, and righteousness in the earth. *For in these I delight"* (emphasis mine). Or, for good measure, I claim Zephaniah 3:17, "The Lord your God in your midst, the Mighty One, will save; He will rejoice over you with gladness, He will quiet you in His love, He will rejoice over you with singing."

When I feel alone in some cause, I let the Spirit remind me, "For He Himself has said, 'I will never leave you nor forsake you'" (Hebrews 13:5). Or, "Lo, I am with you always" (Matthew 28:20).

In times of temptation of any kind, I grasp the sword of the Spirit spoken through the apostle John: "He who is in you is greater than he who is in the world" (1 John 4:4); or, through the apostle Paul, "No temptation has overtaken you except such as is common to man; but God is faithful, who will not allow you to be tempted beyond what you are able, but with the temptation will also make the way of escape, that you may be able to bear it" (1 Corinthians 10:13); or, through the author of Hebrews speaking of Christ, "For in that He Himself has suffered, being tempted, He is able to aid those who are tempted" (Hebrews 2:18).

∼

When I feel alone in some cause, I let the Spirit remind me, "For He Himself has said, 'I will never leave you nor forsake you.'" **Hebrews 13:5**

∼

The treasure chest of God's inspired Word is bottomless. There's a promise for every situation and enough for every day of the rest of our lives.

DISCERNING AND SUITED UP FOR BATTLE

With the Holy Spirit's help, we need to get suited up with the whole armor of God each day and ask for the gift of discernment. Paul reminds us this happens in prayer: "Praying always with all prayer and supplication in the Spirit, being watchful to this end with all perseverance and supplication for all the saints" (Ephesians 6:18). This quality of prevailing prayer is prompted and guided by the Holy Spirit. He shows us the enemy and prepares us for the day's battle.

I like to imagine my divine Armorbearer suiting me up. Then, when I'm fully dressed for battle, He hands me the sword of truth. "You'll not be alone," He says. "I'll be there with you to help you see things as they are, so you will not be duped by Satan. I'll give you a word of Scripture I've inspired, and empower you with the courage to speak and take your stand." Who'd want to face the battle without that kind of preparation? So decide now to put on the full armor of God this day and every day. Your divine Discerner and Armorbearer is always there to help you.

Do you really believe that? Can we really trust our Counselor always to be there? So often people express their fear of losing the Holy Spirit. Is our fellowship with Him an "on again, off again" kind of relationship? Once we become His counselees does He ever discharge us? Does He ever give up on us? For the answer to these haunting questions, turn the page.

10) Can We Ever Lose the Holy Spirit?

W HAT IS YOUR GREATEST FEAR? There's no doubt about how David, Israel's mighty king, would have answered. "Lord, do not cast me away from Your presence. And do not take your Holy Spirit from me."

Does that ever happen? Can we ever lose the Holy Spirit?

David's worst fear of losing the Holy Spirit was based on both positive and negative experiences. When he was a young man he had been anointed by Samuel. With that anointing, the shepherd was given the supernatural power of the Spirit. He became a charismatic lodestar leader of others. His personality became magnetic and inspiring. He did spectacular things as a warrior and king of Israel. Reading his psalms of praise and supplication, we know David gave God the glory, and therefore, the flow of the Holy Spirit was persistent and consistent in his times of deepest need. Why, then, would he fear that the Spirit would be taken from him?

It was an educated fear. David had observed the tragic

thing that had happened to King Saul. Repeatedly, Saul expressed his unwillingness follow the guidance of the Spirit communicated through the prophet Samuel. Finally, the obdurate king was given what he wanted: he didn't want God to rule his life! The Scriptures say the Spirit departed from Saul. In reality, long before, Saul departed from the Spirit. He was willful to the end, even as he fell on his own sword in imperious self-destruction.

David never forgot what happened to Saul. From his understanding of the workings of the Spirit, he assumed that he had departed from Saul. "O God, don't ever let that happen to me!" was his heartfelt cry.

Then David committed a sin that brought him to the edge of the abyss of self-condemnation. His greatest fear was what he thought, in his own estimation, he deserved. "Lord, don't do it—don't take your Holy Spirit from me!"

◦∾

David never forgot what happened to Saul. From his understanding of the workings of the Spirit, he assumed that he had departed from Saul. "O God, don't ever let that happen to me!" was his heartfelt cry.

◦∾

David has been called the greatest saint and the greatest sinner of the Old Testament. He was certainly both. The latter happened in a moment of lust and passion, followed by a dastardly deed. He stole Bathsheba from Uriah, one of his faithful soldiers, committed adultery with her, and then by a clever intrigue, contrived to have Uriah killed in battle so he could take Bathsheba as his wife.

But God knew what the king had done. His omniscience was imparted to the prophet Nathan, who went to David. Nathan told the king a simple parable about a rich man and a poor man. The poor man had only one little lamb and the rich man stole it from him.

David burst out with anger. "Whoever would do that? Who is that man?" With a rapier thrust of truth, Nathan said, "You are the man!"

∽

The prayer that poured forth from David's distraught soul is recorded for us as Psalm 51. At the center of it is the anguished cry, "Do not take Your Holy Spirit from me!"

∽

The king of Israel knew that the moment he had feared all of his life had come. In a time of temptation, he had done the thing he thought he would never do, and had multiplied his sin with an act of treachery he had never imagined he could do. He also knew that he was accountable to God. It was the one thread that held him from falling into the abyss.

Filled with panic, David put on sackcloth and ashes and repented. The prayer that poured forth from his distraught soul is recorded for us as Psalm 51. At the center of it is the anguished cry, "Do not take Your Holy Spirit from me!"

David knew that he could not exist, much less remain as king, without the Holy Spirit. Take anything away from me— my power, my armies—but don't take away the Holy Spirit! David knew that without the Holy Spirit he was nothing. Talent was not enough. His own ingenious methods of leadership wouldn't suffice. His accumulation of wealth would not help him. Only the Holy Spirit could enable him to remain as king of Israel. Take not your Holy Spirit from me!

But listen again. Wasn't this cry of panic an enormous transference to God of his own self-condemning heart? Wasn't David projecting to the Almighty what, in his judgment, he deserved? He could not imagine that God would forgive him and continue to bless him. What would he do if he were God? The king had already expressed that in his reaction to what the rich man had done in Nathan's parable. And now it was he. Indeed, he was the man. Would God's mercy outdistance the judgment David would have decreed for David? Hope against hope. Take not your Holy Spirit from me!

WHAT ABOUT US TODAY?

Now back to you and me. Can this dreadful thing happen? Is there ever a time when God decides to take away the Holy Spirit from those who have not obeyed or done His will—who have refused to love as He has loved them? Does God's patience ever run out?

In the light of all we've said about the Holy Spirit as the greatest Counselor in the world, can we imagine that He would be unavailable because of something we might say or do? Could we neglect consistent counseling sessions with Him and one day call out and find He is no longer there? If He has given us guidance and we have refused to follow it, does there ever come a time when He refuses to help us? When we misuse His power does He ever become exasperated and leave us to flounder on our own?

Before we can answer these questions, we need to confront some very basic misconceptions.

The first misconception. The first misconception is that the Holy Spirit is given on the basis of human merit. Instead of thinking of the Holy Spirit as a sovereign, tri-equal Person of the Trinity, we think of Him as an extra given to believers who are good enough or have discovered the right formula for experiencing the luxury of the joy and power of the Holy Spirit, in addition to their salvation. This misses the prevenient, beforehand ministry of the Holy Spirit who prepared us for salvation and made it possible for us to confess Christ as Lord.

This idea that the Holy Spirit is perceived as an added accolade for the deserving is expressed so often. People say to me,

"Well, I've never received the Holy Spirit. You see, I'm not holy enough yet. I have to get my life in order. Someday, maybe...." Some Spirit-filled Christians help perpetuate this myth. The subtle implication given is that they are the chosen darlings of the Almighty and that their esoteric status was somehow merited by them. Their extolling of the victorious, triumphant life—while at the same time, leaving out how the Holy Spirit had to form and mold them through the years—often gives the impression of a super-saint superiority. What's communicated is like the Marine Corps' recruiting motto, "Only if you're good enough!"

The second misconception. The real danger of thinking that the Holy Spirit fills us on the basis of human merit is the second misconception. It's really the flipside of the first. We think the Holy Spirit is removed because of human failure. I hear people say, "Well, I had the Holy Spirit once, but I lost Him." Do we realize what we're saying? We never *have* the Holy Spirit, as if He were our possession. He has us. A man said to me, "I've really gotten ahold of the Holy Spirit!" I replied, "Don't you mean the Holy Spirit has taken ahold of you?"

~

Though the Holy Spirit never closes us off, we do have the capability of closing Him off. He doesn't leave us, but our sense of His presence is shut off by our resistance to Him.

~

The Holy Spirit plays for keeps. He is faithful. He shares the indefatigable love of the heart of the Father and the pursuing grace of the Son. When we think we are the biggest sinners alive, He can handle it. What's dangerous is the veiled arrogance of thinking our inadequacies or failures can control the Holy Spirit. Our transference to Him of what we'd do to ourselves if we were God is projection of the worst kind. We usually have so much less patience with ourselves than He has. We say, "If someone did to me what I've done to You, I'd give up on him." God the Holy Spirit does have that option. On this side of Calvary, He chooses not to exercise it.

However, though the Holy Spirit never closes us off, we do have the capability of closing Him off. He doesn't leave us, but our sense of His presence is shut off by our resistance to Him. As I have said previously, we can say "no" to the "Inner Voice" so long that there is a time when we lose the desire to say "yes." We can neglect the opportunity to take time with our Counselor and begin to run things on our own. We may run headlong into a big crisis and, in the midst of it, feel what we think is the absence of the Spirit. But it's really the emptiness He's allowed us to experience to bring us back to Him as our Guide and Strength. Or we may follow a path that He has not willed and actually cautioned us against, and wake up to a disaster that seems like punishment for disobedience. The Holy Spirit has then allowed us what we wanted: our own hands-on management of our lives and His noninterfering, hands-off, lack of control.

I spent a long time recently with a man who has been a strong lay leader in his church. He was deeply involved in church work and in getting ahead in his profession. He was married and had three lovely daughters. Though he once was in a close counseling relationship with the Holy Spirit, he had drifted away from daily prayer counseling sessions. One day he became aware of his strong attraction to a beautiful woman several years younger than his wife. He tried to rationalize that there was something wrong with his wife. If she had been more of what he needed, he would not have been sexually aroused by this younger woman. In his heart of hearts, he knew this was not the real problem. In reality, he was simply infatuated. He also knew that he should confess the problem to the Holy Spirit and get help, but he knew he could never get permissive approval from the Spirit for what he was feeling for the young woman and she obviously was now feeling for him.

That's when the drift away from both consistent prayer and fellowship with other Christian men began. He set himself up for what eventually happened. A pregnant woman, an estranged wife, three ashamed daughters, and a shocked church that he had helped build and lead for several years. He came to see me because his own pastor was too disappointed and angry with him to try to help.

The man's opening remarks were, "I feel like I've lost the Holy Spirit!" After he told me the mess he was in, I said, "My friend, you have not lost the Holy Spirit, you have turned your back on Him, closed your mind to His guidance, and shut the ears of your heart to His 'Inner Voice.' You knew you could not get His approval. He is never permissive when it comes to righteousness and holy living. You knew that and cut off communications. But Christ has not drummed you out of the corps and the Holy Spirit is ready to help you do what real love demands. You need to cease from your own willful departure from moral integrity, repent with full confession, and return to a submissive dependence on the Holy Spirit to show you how to deal with the results of what you have done."

When the man finally was ready to get on his knees to pray, the Holy Spirit was there, breaking the bondage, seeking to set him free and reveal the costly restitution that was ahead. Good thing. He needed the Holy Spirit that evening more than ever. In his letters he tells me that day by day the Holy Spirit is helping him unravel the terrible mess he created.

Sometimes our failures or willful sins are not as obvious as this man's were. We hide them from others; and, absurd as it is, we think we can hide them from the Holy Spirit. We know what happens in a human relationship when we try to cover up something we know will give pain and hurt to a person. Ever notice that after you've been overly critical about a person or gossiped about him or her—or actually manipulated some circumstances that will eventually bring trouble in his or her life—you feel strained when you are with that person? The same thing happens in our relationship with the Holy Spirit.

WILL WE LIVE IN SIN OR BY HOLY SPIRIT POWER?

Homing pigeon sins. There's an account of a strange crime that was reported in the *London Times* years ago. A lady found on her doorstop a basket that contained a pigeon. An attached note said that if the woman did not fasten a certain amount of money to the clip on the pigeon's leg and release the bird immediately, her house would be burned down that night. The lady called the police. Wisely, the police officers released the pigeon and, by means of an airplane, traced its course to a house where they found two men whom they arrested. The men pled innocence, saying the bird was not theirs. "All right," the officers said, "we'll test it out." They took the pigeon a long distance away and again released it. It flew back to the same house. The test was repeated several times. The extortioners finally broke down and confessed.

~

Anything we resist letting the Spirit help us confess to the Savior will eventually bring us to the place where we feel He's left us.

~

Think of the homing pigeons of our deeds that keep coming back! We can't get rid of them. We hope no one knows. But we know that the Holy Spirit knows. Sometimes our relationship with Him is blocked because we understand all too well His omniscience. He's close at hand when the pigeons come home to roost in our uneasy minds. Anything we resist letting Him help us confess to the Savior will eventually bring us to the place where we feel He's left us. In actuality, He's not the one who left.

Living on Artesian Power. Most frequently, a sense of the absence of the Holy Spirit is that we are trying to live on our own energy. There's a wonderful story told by A.J. Gordon. He was taking a long walk one afternoon. He looked across a field and saw a farmhouse with a pump nearby in the yard. There was a man vigorously and rhythmically pumping the pump. Gordon stood at a distance watching in amazement for a half hour. The water flowed out of the pump continuously, the man's rhythmic pumping never varied.

Gordon said to himself, "How can this be? How can that man go on pumping so long?" Finally, he walked across the field into the farmyard and up to the pump. It was then that he discovered that a manlike mannequin was tied to the pump, and the water was flowing from an artesian well!

$\sim$

When we try to pump the resources from ourselves, life becomes difficult. And we can't ever pump the Holy Spirit! But we can be pumped by Him.

$\sim$

To me, that's a parable of the Spirit-filled life. When we try to pump the resources from ourselves, life becomes difficult. And we can't ever pump the Holy Spirit! But we can be pumped by Him, not as a lifeless mannequin, but as a person through whom the artesian power of the Holy Spirit was meant to flow.

Can we lose the Holy Spirit? No. Not now. Not ever. But there are ways we can keep open to His ever-present help as our Counselor.

PAUL'S TWO ADMONITIONS

The apostle Paul has given us two admonitions that are very clear and need to be remembered. The first was to the church at Thessalonica: "Do not quench the Spirit." Now, what comes before and after that admonition is very important. As a matter of fact, all the verses in that fifth chapter of 1 Thessalonians, from the sixteenth verse to the twenty-second verse, are crucial for understanding how the Holy Spirit works in our lives and what happens to us when we are in the stream of His power. If we take the admonition "Do not quench the Spirit" as the fulcrum of the whole passage, we begin to see the description of truly serendipitous living. "Rejoice always. Pray without ceasing. In everything give thanks; for this is the will of God in Christ Jesus for you. Do not quench the Spirit." In other words, refusing to rejoice always, pray constantly, and in all things give thanks is the way that we create resistance to the Holy Spirit and eventually end up feeling as if the Holy Spirit has departed from us.

~

"Rejoice always. Pray without ceasing. In everything give thanks; for this is the will of God in Christ Jesus for you. Do not quench the Spirit." 1 Thessalonians 5:16-19

~

The word "quench" in the Greek means "to dampen." The Holy Spirit is the fire of God in us. How do you put out a fire? Two ways. You douse it with water, or you just neglect it. Eventually, if you don't feed a fire, it won't grow. It loses its glow. The opposite of quenching is to fuel the fire in our hearts by rejoicing, actually praising God in the midst of all circumstances. Praying constantly is making all of life a companionship with the Lord. It means that bringing Him into every circumstance and every relationship, and then giving thanks in the midst of everything, is the way we experience release from the stress and tension of our own control.

The Holy Spirit gives us this power. When difficulties come, He helps us say, "Thank you, Lord. There's something that I'm going to discover in this I could have never known otherwise." When triumphs come, instead of saying, "Well, I did it," we say, "Lord, thank you. You made it possible."

∼

"Do not grieve the Holy Spirit." This reminds us that the Holy Spirit is a person, otherwise He couldn't grieve.

∼

Quenching the Holy Spirit is refusing to allow the flame to glow brightly. A Christian should be radiant, alive with love. Our eyes are meant to dance with joy. There ought to be such warmth from our countenance that others are drawn magnetically, not just to us, but to the Spirit living in us.

The second admonition of the apostle Paul is in the fourth chapter of his letter to the Ephesians in the thirtieth verse: "Do not grieve the Holy Spirit." This reminds us that the Holy Spirit is a person, otherwise He couldn't grieve. His heart can be broken. He can ache over us. And what is it that grieves Him? The whole passage there in the fourth chapter of Ephesians is about expressing the love and forgiveness that we have received. The Holy Spirit is the power of the Living God in us enabling us to love and forgive, to endure, to persist.

So anytime that you feel the Holy Spirit has departed from you, He hasn't departed; you have. Remember the old question, "If you feel God is absent, who moved?" He doesn't move. He's with us, but He's given us this awesome capacity to say "no." Again, we were created with free will. We can actually say "no" for so long that there comes a time, psychologically and spiritually, when it's very hard to say "yes."

Now you may be on the edge of that. You may have resisted the Spirit so long that you don't want Him anymore. What a tragedy it would be if He gave you what you wanted! Jesus called the persistent blaspheming of the Holy Spirit the only unforgivable sin. It's the sin of resisting the Spirit's influence to help us trust Christ as Lord of all.

But the glorious thing is, if we can cry out, "Lord, cast me not away from your presence, take not your Holy Spirit from me," the assurance is this: at that very moment the Holy Spirit is at work in us, creating in us a desire for life anew in Christ.

~

Can we ever lose the Holy Spirit?
Once more for emphasis: No. Not now. Not ever.

~

Emil Brunner said, "What oxygen is for the lungs, the Holy Spirit is for the soul."

I encourage you to picture, vividly picture, yourself no longer resisting the daily filling of the Holy Spirit. Imagine yourself as free, open, rejoicing, giving thanks, and praying constantly. Picture yourself living in the flow of love for people, even those people you don't think deserve to be forgiven. Envision yourself with supernatural intellectual gifts, emotional powers, physical strength, and moral integrity. Hold that picture! Have you got the image? Can you see yourself? Full of the Holy Spirit? It's your birthright!

Can we ever lose the Holy Spirit? Once more for emphasis: No. Not now. Not ever. Remember that His fruit is patience and kindness. He won't give up on you. So don't give up on your need to keep on being filled with Him!

WHAT CAN WE DO?

Here are some basic things we can do to avoid the dreadful misconception that we have lost the Holy Spirit.

1. *Accept* the truth that the Holy Spirit has taken us on as His counselees for the rest of our lives until we graduate to heaven. He is persistent in His love and is with us at our points of deepest need. Our failures will not cause Him to reject, leave, or forsake us. He will help us overcome repetitive patterns of sins and give us the power to change and be different.

2. *Admit* that at times we do resist the Holy Spirit. Our relationship with the Holy Spirit is a love relationship and sometimes we resist being loved. The moment we feel a strain in our relationship with Him because of what we have said or done, He is lovingly correcting us. He never changes, so we can confess our willful independence or neglect and open the floodgates of our hearts to allow Him to love us. There is no sin too big for Him to deal with by mediating the grace of the cross.

3. *Affirm* that we cannot make it without daily counseling sessions with the Holy Spirit and constant fellowship with Him all through the ups and downs of any day. This affirmation of our need and the Holy Spirit's constant availability to counsel us needs to be put into a fresh commitment. We should never allow a day to go by without time alone with Him.

4. *Act* on the guidance the Holy Spirit gives us. Trust the "Inner Voice" of the Spirit, respond to His nudges. Faithfulness in little things keeps us open to receive His help when the big challenges and opportunities come along.

5. *Accountability* to the Holy Spirit on a daily basis is the secret of spiritual power and growth. That accountability is not a grim duty but a great delight. That's the discovery we're going to make in the next and final chapter about the greatest Counselor in the world.

11) Check the Dailies

A NYONE IN THE FILM INDUSTRY knows the meaning of a director's admonition at the end of a day of shooting movie scenes. "Check the dailies!" the director says as he or she calls it a day. For the cinematographer and the film development lab, the day's work has just begun and it may go on all night.

"Dailies" is a term for the footage that has been filmed in any one day. It's crucial for the cinematographer to develop the film, so the director can see what was done during the day. These are also called "rushes." The name implies what they are: developed film rushed to the director for review. When he or she sees them, the director will know what might need to be redone, what needs improvement in the next day's shooting, and how what was done in any one day fits into the overall drama of the finished movie.

Were the cameras all in focus? Were there any distortions in the lenses? Was the lighting perfect and in keeping with previous scenes? Was the script followed accurately? Was the performance of the actors up to their best? These are questions the director must ask as he or she checks the "dailies." The director knows they have to be right. He or she is responsible to the producer for the quality of the day's shoot.

One Sunday morning I talked to one of the directors in my congregation in Hollywood. He had a long, dejected face. "What's wrong?" I asked. "I've just checked the dailies of Friday's and Saturday's shooting of the film I'm working on. There was a little hair on one of the camera lenses. The cameraman didn't catch it. We'll have to do it all over."

CHECKING OUR DAILIES

This phrase, "check the dailies," could be a good challenge to a Christian. We are actors in a divine drama. Without pushing the metaphor too far, the Holy Spirit is our director. He's responsible for our performance and is committed to helping us do our best. Christ is our producer, the reigning Lord of the church and the whole Christian movement. He and the Holy Spirit have been given their assignments by the Father, the investor, who has committed His resources to the spreading of His kingdom and righteousness on planet Earth and for the reconciling of humankind to Himself.

~

*We are to live each day as if it were
the only day we have.*

~

Checking the dailies with the Holy Spirit is a vital part of evaluating what we've been and what we've done in our challenging role as disciples. Our life is typically divided into day-tight compartments. We are to live each day as if it were the only day we have. Checking our daily performance is crucial and should include taking our hope and love inventories, donning our spiritual armor and seeking the discernment of the Spirit, and overcoming our yesterdays, as talked about in earlier chapters. Without a daily check, a lousy day may be followed by a bad day, and days mount into months and then years. Unless we allow the Holy Spirit to involve us in an honest, open review of our dailies, we could perpetuate patterns in our performance that, in the end, add up to be a life that is far less than it was intended to be. In fact, as indicated in the last chapter, we can even reach the place where we are no longer receptive to the guidance of the Holy Spirit as our Counselor and are tempted to falsely believe that He has deserted us.

Checking the dailies is really taking a decisive look at our "daily living." This term might be more familiar to most of us. We use it for the down-to-earth affairs of life, the things we do, the people we see, the work we do each day. Unfortunately, the term is falsely considered the opposite of times of inspiration when the daily round of things is interrupted by some serendipity. We experience a surprise in the midst of ordinary things, an invasion of delight in the drag of dull days.

Most of us do have a succession of gray days at times, neither bright with excitement nor dimmed by depressing events. So life limps on. Therefore, we come to believe that the opposite is to discover how to "walk in the Spirit." We forget that the Holy Spirit not only wants to, but *can* make a difference in our daily living.

WALKING IN THE SPIRIT

The code word of the Scriptures for daily living is walking. It's used figuratively for the whole round of activities of a person. Paul uses walking as a metonym for life in the Holy Spirit. "Walk in the Spirit," he challenges us in Galatians. "If we live in the Spirit, let us also walk in the Spirit" (Galatians 5:16, 25). Being filled by the Spirit daily, we are to live in His power, be open to His guidance, and be led by His "Inner Voice." Through the generations the term "daily walk" has been synonymous with this companionship and communion with the Holy Spirit as our Counselor.

∾

Being filled by the Spirit daily, we are to live in His power, be open to His guidance, and be led by His "Inner Voice."

∾

Paul also drew on his own experience with the Holy Spirit when he encouraged the Ephesians to walk as "children of light" and to "walk circumspectly, not as fools but as wise, redeeming the time, because the days are evil" (Ephesians 5:8, 15-16). The word "redeeming" means "buying." We are to buy up the time, says Paul urgently. He implies that we purchase the minutes and hours of each day by using them to the fullest.

The Holy Spirit is also head of our purchasing department. He shows us how to make the most of each day. As the director of the drama of the autobiography of our lives being lived and recorded each day, He is in charge of maximizing our performance and seeing that we enjoy the unfolding drama as it evolves. He's particularly concerned that we never lose sight of the purpose of each day, and in the light of that, how we begin the day, how we draw on His strength for the challenges of the day, and how we end the day checking the dailies. All this is part of walking in the Spirit—each day.

The purpose of our daily walk. I'm not talking about a morning walk for exercise, though many of us have found that to be an important part of keeping fit physically. Rather, I'm talking about what happens when we first wake up. Walking in the Spirit requires a daily decision that needs to be made as we greet each day. Our early morning counseling session with the greatest Counselor in the world is not just important; it's absolutely essential.

Some people call this their "quiet time" or their daily devotional time. I call it daily morning worship. The Holy Spirit calls us to worship. He involves us in what we've referred to as the glory circle. We are caught up in the Holy Spirit's glorification of Christ, are drawn by the praise of the Son into the very heart of the Father. As we've said, worship is not something we do from a distance, but a glorious experience we share with the Persons of the Trinity. Then we are led to confession, prayers for others, and specific supplication for the challenges of the day ahead. Reading a portion of Scripture each morning feeds our hungry souls. Then we are ready to focus the Spirit's goals for the day and commit ourselves to them.

~

*Our early morning counseling session with the greatest
Counselor in the world is not just important;
it's absolutely essential.*

~

The Holy Spirit sets before us the purpose of any day. Remember His role is to help us glorify Christ *and* serve Him. He reminds us of our daily motto from the Master: "If anyone desires to come after Me, let him deny himself, take up his cross daily, and follow Me" (Luke 9:23, emphasis mine). It's perilous to begin any day without a fresh commitment to Christ's calling. But what does it mean?

Our cross is not some physical malady or difficult person or problematic situation as some imply when they say with resignation, "Well, I guess that's my cross!" Taking up our cross means to be a servant regardless of what it costs. It's obedience to be to others what Christ has been to us. And it involves sacrificial love spelled out in costly ways of giving our-

186 / The Greatest Counselor in the World

selves away in loving, forgiving, helping, encouraging, affirming, and caring, even when we don't feel like it.

Here's the salient point: we are to make a conscious decision to be a servant each day. When we let one morning go by without an intentional commitment to our daily cross, it will make that day unfocused and begin a blur through the days ahead. Weeks later we'll be jolted by some crisis and wonder what happened to our spiritual lives.

STRENGTH IS FOR SERVICE!

The open secret of a dynamic walk in the Spirit is this: *The Holy Spirit's strength is for service.* Being filled daily by the Spirit is not *just* for our enjoyment or warm fuzzy feelings, or even our private piety. The Holy Spirit wants to equip us for ministry. Every day. His gifts of love, wisdom, faith, knowledge, discernment, healing, and prophecy to speak forth boldly about our faith—all are given as empowering for our daily cross of service. The fruit of the Spirit, the character manifestations of the indwelling Holy Spirit, are to make us effective in our relationships. When the Spirit grows in us the fruit of love, joy, peace, long-suffering, kindness, goodness, faithfulness, gentleness, and self-control—that fruit is not given to make us spiritually well-dressed models for a fashion show, but for life in the tough, grubby, demanding trenches that demarcate the battlefield of daily life. There's a tremendous release when we begin to think that a really good day is one in which we've been used to make a difference in the lives of people around us.

Denying ourselves is the crucifixion of our desire to control our own lives. Daily denial of self is simply putting Christ and other people ahead of ourselves in our agenda for any day. It's not getting rid of the self. The self is the riverbed for the flow of the Spirit. At the beginning of the day, we only know part of what's ahead. Even in what we know about, there will be interruptions by people with needs. And what we don't know about the day is that it may have some major crisis we had not scheduled into our careful planning. *But in each crisis there will be an opportunity to serve.*

The Holy Spirit gets us ready. A part of His assignment is to bring to our remembrance at the beginning of the day what Christ has said. He echoes what Christ said after He washed the disciples' feet. "Do you know what I have done to you? You call me Teacher and Lord, and you say well, for so I am. If I then, your Lord and Teacher, have washed your feet, you also ought to wash one another's feet. For I have given you an example, that you should do as I have done to you. Most assuredly, I say to you, a servant is not greater than his master; nor is he who is sent greater than he who sent him. If you know these things, happy are you if you do them" (John 13:12-17).

When we are willing to make a fresh commitment each morning to be a servant, then the Holy Spirit gives us some powerful reassurances from Scripture. "As your days, so will your strength be" (Deuteronomy 33:25). That promise is backed up by His faithfulness.

◊

"May I know Thee more clearly, love Thee more dearly, follow Thee more nearly."

◊

So at the beginning of each day, we can say with Jeremiah, "This I will recall to mind, therefore I have hope. Through the Lord's mercies we are not consumed, because his compassions fail not. They are new every morning; great is your faithfulness" (Lamentations 3:21-23). And then we can claim this, "I [God] will never leave you nor forsake you" (Hebrews 13:5).

Richard of Chichester gave us words to pray in response.

Steven Schwartz set them to music as part of the musical *Godspell.* "May I know Thee more clearly, love Thee more dearly, follow Thee more nearly." Schwartz appropriately added the words, "Day by day, day by day." I'd say, "Today, Lord, today!"

THE CAMERAS ARE ROLLING!

Throughout the day, the cameras are rolling, recording how we live out our calling to be servants. The Holy Spirit keeps a record of the day's events, not to incriminate us but to help us make the next day even better. Knowing that adds intensity to life. What we do and say in any one day does matter! And all through the day the Holy Spirit is communicating with His "Inner Voice." "This is the way; walk in it" (Isaiah 30:21).

One Sunday morning, I got up at five to go down to my study to finish memorizing my sermon. It just so happened that I was going to share some of the content in this chapter with my congregation. As I drove to the church, I prayed, "Holy Spirit, I need a fresh anointing of Your power. Breathe life into the words that I've prepared. Give me a deeper awareness of what it means to be interruptible and ready to serve."

I didn't expect this prayer to be answered before I reached my study! On the way, I stopped at a 7-Eleven convenience store that's open all night. As I got out of my car, I was approached by, not one, but six beggars who were lurking in the shadows near the entrance of this store waiting to beg for a handout from customers. Usually they take turns, rotating who would get the next prospect. Instead, they all descended on me at once, each trying to jostle ahead of the other, raising his voice above the rest while shouting out a carefully rehearsed appeal.

One pled for money for a cup of coffee; I thought of the full breakfast I had just eaten. Another claimed that his car was out of gas and he couldn't get home; I looked at my fine automobile full of gas. Still another, who looked more sophisticated than the rest, complained that he had lost his job and had taken to the streets; I thought of the privilege of working at a fine job that day.

And so it went, until the chorus of human misery was finished. I reached in my pocket and felt the dollar bills I had scooped off my dresser earlier before leaving home, not counting how many there were. With my fingers in my pocket, I counted them. Six bills, no change! What to do? "Even as you have done it to the least of these...." I hear you, Lord! I pulled out all six dollar bills and gave one to each man. They all faded back into the shadows. No need to go into the store. I had no money.

As I turned to get back into my car, one of the men called out from the shadows, "Thank you, Dr. Ogilvie...." He knew who I was! I had come so close to being disgruntled with these men. After all, I needed to get to church to get ready to preach on servanthood! The Holy Spirit had answered my prayer in a way I had not expected. I thank Him that I paid attention.

Yes, the cameras were rolling, recording one event of a long day that would be part of my dailies. And so was the conversation I had with the man who shouted from the shadows. I was a well-dressed beggar on the way to his study talking to another beggar about where to find bread... real Bread!

There are people around all of us who are not homeless, but who need to be "at home" with the Father, who have three square meals a day and yet are spiritually hungry, who know a lot about many things and yet do not really know the Savior, who wield great personal power, but desperately need the power of the Holy Spirit. The cameras also are rolling as we relate to them, as well as loved ones who need our affirmation and encouragement. Sometimes the people closest to us express their needs in ways that tempt us to react to their method of getting our attention, rather than responding to their need for someone to listen in a patient, nonjudgmental way. How do we respond? Do we call upon the Spirit for counsel and power when we need him?

When people get on our nerves. Recently, a friend showed me two cartoons that first made me laugh and then made me think. One depicted a woman in terrible disarray. Her hair was frazzled in a stringy mess. Under her eyes were big, dark bags. Her face was lined, her mouth was turned down, and her eyes expressed a "How could you?" look. The words at the bottom of the cartoon went like this: "When I woke up this morning I had one nerve left and now you're getting on it!" Ever feel that way? Do people ever get on your nerves?

~

It's when people do get on our nerves and life gets pressured that we have an opportunity to take specific steps in our "walk in the Spirit."

~

The other cartoon was one from Mankoff, the *New Yorker* magazine cartoonist's inimitable drawing pen. It showed a harried businessman behind a desk covered with papers. The man was holding a phone to his ear with one hand, while with the other he leafed through his appointment book. He said, "No, Thursday's out. How about never—is never good for you?" Ever wish you could say that when life gets jammed up and stress boils inside?

It's when people do get on our nerves and life gets pressured that we have an opportunity to take specific steps in our "walk in the Spirit." The Holy Spirit walks with us, but He also talks to us. Paul distinguished the immense difference between walking by the flesh and walking in the Spirit.

"Flesh" means our own human nature limited to our own strength and sagacity. Walking in the Spirit is drawing on the divine energy and knowledge. He gives us a "word of knowledge." It is His distinctive gift.

More profound than human insight or analysis, it is specific revelation about not only what's really happening in people and situations, but what is needed to fulfil what the Lord wants at that moment in time. Further, it's usually clear direction for a practical way to live out the call to deny ourselves and take up the cross. We are to walk "in newness of life" (Romans 6:4) as new creatures in Christ, not in the old nature that demands that we be number one.

A woman who is an elder in my congregation is a good example of this. Evelyn could use her elevated position of authority and power in the congregation for her own aggrandizement. Instead, she is a servant. She is a role model for many young women whom she prays and cares for by being available to listen and give practical help. Her life is saturated with the Holy Spirit. As a result, she sees beneath the surface of things and can share with empathy what the Spirit puts on her heart for people. She takes part in the prayer and healing ministry of the elders at the conclusion of our services. When she prays for people, it is with the gift of knowledge of the deeper problems beneath people's expressed needs. Often these people say to me, "How did she know? She went right for the hidden hurt in me without my telling her. Amazing!"

A distinguished lawyer I know is like the Barnabas of New Testament times. He's a "son of encouragement." His immense intelligence, coupled with the knowledge of people and situations birthed in him by the Holy Spirit, enables him to care for hundreds of people. His widespread network of friends enjoys the encouragement this man expresses so winsomely. I'm privileged to be part of that network and countless times have received his on-time calls or visits just when I needed them most. He always seems to know what to say and it's on target. "John," I ask, "How did you know that I needed you today and how in the world did you know how to put your finger on that raw nerve?"

Recently, when a lonely old actor in our congregation endured a long illness before dying, John visited him every day. The actor had no family and his dying months became very difficult for him. John never gave up. He arranged for his hospitalization, cared for his finances, reminded others to call him, and helped the man die with dignity. Why? Because John is a servant. With the knowledge of the Holy Spirit, he saw beneath the actor's polished exterior to the loneliness of a once well-known actor with one hundred and twenty movies to his credit, who felt the world had forgotten him.

Then I think of a successful banker named Fred who is very effective in sharing his faith because he sees into people with the X-ray penetration of the knowledge given him by the Holy Spirit. One evening a week he calls on people who have visited our church. Recently I received a letter from a father in Texas. His daughter is a college freshman who has been attending our church in Hollywood. He expressed delight in how his daughter had been cared for by an elder in my church. I knew it was Fred. The young woman had indicated on her registration slip in worship that she would like to talk with someone about her faith. When Fred visited her, he discerned that though she had been raised in a church back home, she needed to make a personal commitment to Christ and receive the Holy Spirit. During Fred's visit with her, she found the joy and assurance she needed because Fred had the gift of discernment to see her real need and deal with it with sensitivity and empathy.

Fred never touts his title in the banking world. He does not draw attention to himself or need recognition for his lay ministry. He simply walks in the light and truth of Christ and is gifted by the Holy Spirit to quietly press on helping people live abundantly and forever.

Walking in the light and in the truth. The apostle John talked about walking in the light (1 John 1:7) and walking in the truth (3 John 3). The two are parts of the same thing. Christ is our light. He promised that those who follow Him will not walk in darkness. In His light we see truth, live the truth, and speak the truth. And the Holy Spirit is the inner light who helps us know exactly what that is for each relationship and circumstance.

~

"If we walk in the light as He is in the light, we have fellowship with one another." 1 John 1:7

~

Walking in the light is the only possible basis of true fellowship. John puts it clearly, "If we walk in the light as He is in the light, we have fellowship with one another" (1 John 1:7). Nothing debilitates deep relationship more than pretense. Often we project a pretend person to others. To try to pretend that we are more or less than we are brings stiffness and strain in our relationships. Others either pretend with us or are put off. Walking in the light shows us who we really are, not just in our weaknesses, but also in our security in Christ. The key to great relationships is vulnerability, letting people know us as growing, sometimes failing, but Spirit-motivated people. Thus, the camera is rolling on the depth of our relationships with other Christians all through the day.

I think of Anna and Jack. They are a twentieth-century reproduction of Priscilla and Aquila, the couple in the book of Acts who did so much to help Paul and the fellowship of the early church. Jack and Anna live simply so they can have more to give away to help individuals and the missionary outreach of the church. They have been seasoned by many years of fellowship with the Holy Spirit. Their knowledge of the Scriptures is both profound and extensive, yet they are eager to learn more. Highly intelligent, both have had successful careers in the academic world—Anna teaching English in high school and Jack, a professor at the University of California. Christ-esteem engendered by the Holy Spirit has given them a joyous confidence. They are at home with people from all levels of society and share their faith with equal ease at their tennis club or with street people and every kind of person in between.

Jack and Anna exemplify creative vulnerability. Their excitement about growing in Christ comes across as true humility. Because they don't give the superior impression of having arrived, they can enter into the struggles of others and, with the gift of discernment, see their needs and help them. Though they have had no children of their own, over the years they have become a spiritual mom and dad to hundreds of teenagers and young adults whom they have helped to walk in the light and truth of Christ.

∽

We may sing "Amazing Grace," but in our daily relationships with nonbelievers, there may be little about us that would lead them to think that something really amazing has happened to us.

∽

In our relationship with nonbelievers, Paul says, "Walk in wisdom toward those who are outsiders, redeeming the time. Let your speech always be with grace, seasoned with salt, that you may know how you ought to answer each one" (Colossians 4:5-6). We know that grace means unqualified love, acceptance, and forgiveness, but how is this to be seasoned with salt? Salt adds zest to bland food. There's nothing bland about the grace of the Lord Jesus Christ, but often our communication of it comes across as bland. We may sing "Amazing Grace," but in our daily relationships with nonbelievers, there may be little about us that would lead them to think that something really amazing has happened to us.

Bland, dull, lackluster Christians are a contradiction in

terms. We are to be life-affirming, joyous, positive people in whom others can see what extraordinary things can be done through an ordinary person walking in the Spirit. Our gracious love for people will attract them to us and then to Christ; our zest will show them that the adventure of living in Christ, empowered by the Holy Spirit, is an exciting way to live.

Salt also preserves. When our speech is gracious and seasoned with salt it never gets rotten with gossip or moldy with festered, hostile criticism. Nothing contradicts our witness to a nonChristian more than negativism about others. People long to find a way to handle the problems that come with human relationships. When we put down people, potential Christians are put off. As a man whom a friend of mine is trying to win to Christ put it, "That guy's no better off than I am. Some example he is! People are my number one problem. Why should I take his Christ seriously when He seems to have done so little for his ability to handle people and what he says about them?" Ouch!

In addition to how we live out our faith in the presence of nonbelievers, we also need to ask the Holy Spirit to guide us in how to share our faith with them. Those who are most effective have discovered the importance of being a caring friend. Many Christians are frightened by the word "witnessing." I most prefer "friendship impact" to describe the way to influence others with our faith. Every Christian ought to have a list of at least twelve people he or she would like to introduce to Christ and the power of the Holy Spirit. Our prospect list becomes a sacred prayer list.

In our counseling times with the Holy Spirit, we can review our list name by name. As we think about each person, we can ask the Holy Spirit for that magnificent gift of discernment we've talked about. He will help us discern what's happening to, around, and inside the person. In most cases we also need the fruit of the Spirit in order to be a caring friend who can earn the right, at the appropriate time, to share Christ. With the Holy Spirit in us, we can have just the perfect measure of love, joy, peace, patience, kindness, goodness, faithfulness, gentleness, or self-control in our relationship with the person we want to reach for Christ.

Also, and this is crucial, we can ask the Holy Spirit to guide us in what we are to say, how we are to say it, and when is the most opportune moment to say it. Be sure of this: if we really have been a caring, trustworthy friend, we will have opportunities to talk about what Christ means to us and can mean to the person we're trying to reach. Someone said people are like islands: you have to row around them until you know where to land. The Holy Spirit wants to guide both where we land and what we should say when we land. As mentioned earlier, I've found that when I pray silently while in conversation with a person I'm trying to reach for Christ, the Holy Spirit has an amazing way of giving me the right thing to say that opens the conversation to deeper sharing. The secret of becoming interesting to others is to be interested in what's important to them or troubling them. When we've listened to them, there's a strong possibility they will be willing to listen to us, especially if it's in response to their needs and problems.

Justice issues. The cameras recording our dailies also document our response to the issues of justice swirling around us. Every day we are confronted with the problems of racism, the poor, and the disadvantaged. In my congregation, we call every member into ministry involving both personal evangelism *and* a crucial social issue in our city: the homeless, runaway, disaffected youth who gravitate to Hollywood, AIDS patients, the aged, the jobless, unwed mothers-to-be, and racial tensions of our city. Lay people who are living dynamic lives have the four elements of vital Christianity: an unreserved commitment to Christ, a daily filling of the Holy Spirit, a ministry with individuals seeking to love and care and share their faith, and a direct involvement in at least one of the major issues of social justice in our time.

None of us can become involved in all the soul-sized issues and causes of our time. We were not meant to run off in all directions. What we are meant to do is seek the Holy Spirit's counseling about what is our particular assignment. Again, when we ask, He will give us guidance and a burning passion to work for justice where He deploys us. His power is provided for what He has called us to do.

CHECKING THE DAILIES AT THE END OF THE DAY

We've talked about how to start our daily walk in the Spirit, and how to walk in the Spirit throughout the day, now we need to consider how to end the day with Him in a way that maximizes our next day. Before we retire at night, our prayers should be a careful review with our Director of the dailies from that day's actions, words, and relationships. He rolls the footage in our mind's eye. There's lots for which we can be thankful and give praise. The Holy Spirit affirms us for times we listened to Him and followed the script of taking up our cross. He cheers what we have done in the very best way possible. He encourages us to take delight as we see evidence of growth and maturity.

We also see times we resisted guidance and missed opportunities. The times we failed and missed the mark are disturbing to see. There were also times we were self-centered, refused to serve, and didn't wash feet by listening and caring in practical ways. Our supply of love and patience ran out, and we didn't return to the Giver. There were times we retreated from the spiritual battle where He has stationed us, not wanting to feel the pain or know the anguish around us. There were times when we didn't depend on the Holy Spirit for a fresh supply of hope, and we gave in to anxiety and irritability.

We look with horror at the footage capturing our competi-

tion, jealousy, pride, anger, put-downs, and our constant need
for the upper hand in relationships. Some of our decisions
didn't stand the test of absolute honesty and impeccable
integrity. Various times throughout the day we simply forgot
to utilize the wisdom, knowledge, and discernment the Holy
Spirit tried to communicate through His Inner Voice. We
weren't listening or, when we were, didn't follow orders.

Checking the dailies can be discouraging if we do it alone.
But the Holy Spirit is there. He wants to mediate to us the
encouragement and forgiveness that are ours for the taking.
He's most concerned to give us a good night's rest and a fresh
start when we begin the new day. Those nightly reviews of our
dailies are so important for that. To reword an old poem:

> So I think I know the secret
> Learned from many a troubled way:
> You must check the dailies in the evening
> To maximize the next day.[1]

Daily bread for tomorrow. As we end our day, the Holy
Spirit reminds us of another time Christ used the word "daily."
I think it was prophetic of the ministry of the Holy Spirit. In
the Lord's Prayer, Christ taught us to pray, "Give us this day
our *daily* bread" (Matthew 6:11). I think Christ taught us to
pray that because He foresaw the post-Pentecost age in which
the Holy Spirit would be the answer to that prayer in more
than simply physical bread.

The Greek word for "daily" in Christ's call to take up our
cross daily is *hēméran*, a daily act. The adjective "daily" in the
petition in the Lord's Prayer is distinctly different. It is *epi-
ousion*, a combination of *epi*—"upon"; and *eimi*—"to be." So
we are to pray for bread for what's to be. Bread for going on
or bread for the morrow. "Give us today the bread we need
for tomorrow."

In the context of the thrust of what we've been saying,

checking the dailies in the evening leads us to pray for strength in facing tomorrow. Who of us can let go of what we've seen about today and sleep with any restfulness unless we have confidence that we have been given the resources to face tomorrow? Christ is the Bread of Life and through the Holy Spirit gives us what we need if we're the least bit open. At the end of a day after we've reviewed the dailies, gently the Holy Spirit whispers, "Now go to sleep. All you need to know is that I'll give you a new day and show you the best way." We can fall asleep with the prayer, "Lord, thank you for the bread tonight that will strengthen me tomorrow. Tomorrow will be different. You'll be the same; but I'll be different."

When I end a day like that, often the words of an old song waft through my mind most of the night:

> I can hear the Savior calling
> "Take up your cross and follow Me."
> He will give me grace and glory,
> And go with me all the way.
> Where He leads me I will follow
> I'll go with Him all the way.[2]

We can be sure that's a prayer the Holy Spirit is always ready to answer.

You see, the Holy Spirit doesn't just check the dailies. He also checks the heavenlies, the vision of you and me making it through this life and successfully into heaven. Our dailies might show some failures, but in accomplishing His ultimate task with us, He never fails.

CONCLUSION

Throughout the pages of this book, I have made some awesome promises to you about what the Holy Spirit can mean to you as your Counselor. These promises are backed up by the Bible, the testimony of Christians through the ages, and the most exciting discoveries of my own experience. Writing this book has been like carrying on a conversation with you, a cherished, valued friend. I've tried to imagine the expression on your face as you've read. I've listened for your questions, your request for further explanation, or for an illustration to paint the word picture more vividly. Then I have written in response.

~

Right now the Holy Spirit is offering to be your personal Counselor—to help you with all your problems, relationships, decisions, and whatever robs you of joy and peace.

~

Now as we conclude our conversation about the greatest Counselor in the world, I wish the two of us were alone together so we could encourage each other in our response to the astounding offers the Holy Spirit is making to both of us.

I want that to happen as you read these closing lines. Right now the Holy Spirit is offering to be your personal Counselor—to help you with all your problems, relationships, decisions, and whatever robs you of joy and peace in the rough and tumble of the asphalt jungle of living today. Think of it! He is ready to press the seal of Christ's image into your character, make you like Him, and help you glorify and serve Him. Just imagine! He promises to enable you to know and do God's will. Sense the wonder of it! The Holy Spirit can be the "Inner Voice" whispering on-the-spot, momentary guidance. Claim it. He will help you know what and how to pray in your greatest struggles. He will empower you with the gift of faith, engender hope, and enliven you with ability to love people profoundly. Feel it! You don't need to battle insecurity and lack of self-esteem any longer. The Holy Spirit communicates to you your personal worth and how much you are loved and cherished by the Father through Christ. Sense the relief! You can overcome your yesterdays, your worry about the future and live each day to the fullest. Every day you can be an overcomer in spiritual warfare because the Holy Spirit will equip you with discernment and suit you up with the whole armor of God. Fear need no longer shackle you with panic. The Holy Spirit will never leave or forsake you. And rejoice! Daily accountability to the Holy Spirit assures you that you can face your mistakes and make a fresh start each morning.

That review of what the Holy Spirit seeks to be for us leads to what now sounds like an absurd question. Knowing what we now know about the power of the Holy Spirit, who would *not* want to trust Him as his or her Counselor? "Not I," I hear you say. So say I!

But knowing us humans, I also realize that we must make the second biggest commitment of our lives if we really mean that. The first is to Christ as our Lord and Savior. Now the second, without which the first has little meaning, is to reorient our priorities and schedules to take time every day with the Holy Spirit, so He can accomplish His magnificent work in us as our Counselor. Knowing human nature as I do, I surmise that oughts and guilt won't motivate us for the long haul. Realizing what the Holy Spirit has waiting for us each day will draw us to our dynamic, liberating, life-changing counseling sessions with Him.

If you have never trusted the Holy Spirit as your Counselor, I invite you to begin with a ninety-day experiment. Each morning and evening bring Him your deepest needs and urgent questions and allow Him to guide, mold, and encourage you. Let Him fill you with faith, hope, love, courage, and confidence. I guarantee you that if you commit yourself to be a counselee of the Holy Spirit for three months, it will change your life and you'll want to continue the rest of your life, never missing your daily appointment.

And those of us who have made a start? My prayer is that what we have said about the Holy Spirit as our Counselor will renew your commitment to daily time with Him. Quite honestly, writing this book has done that for me. As I look back over the years there have been difficult and challenging days, but my only bad days were those when I tried to make it on my own without the power and guidance of the Holy Spirit.

So I join you in this commitment. "Reigning Christ, thank You for sending the Holy Spirit, Your abiding presence with me and in me. In response I confess that I need the Holy Spirit, and I want to make a commitment to be a counselee of the Holy Spirit. Every morning and evening I want to open myself completely to His power and guidance, to His gifts of faith, hope, and love. And now, Holy Spirit, I'm Yours. I want to keep on being filled with You. Manifest Your fruit in me. Mold me, challenge me, change me, use me so that I may fulfill Your plan for me—to glorify, serve, and be made like Christ. I entrust my life to you."

Nothing can ever be the same again for us. We are under the care of the greatest Counselor in the world!

Notes

ONE
The Greatest Counselor in the World

1. G. Campbell Morgan, *The Acts of the Apostles* (Old Tappan, NJ: Fleming H. Revell Co., 1924), 31-32.
2. Thomas F. Torrance, *The Mediation of Christ* (Edinburgh: T. and T. Clark, 1992), 117, 118-19. This book is highly recommended for further study of the Trinity, particularly chapter 5, "The Atonement and the Holy Trinity."

TWO
Sealed by the Spirit

1. E. Stanley Jones, *A Song of Ascents: A Spiritual Autobiography* (Nashville, TN.: Abingdon Press, 1968), 28.
2. Jones, 53.
3. Jones, 53.

THREE
Our Counselor's Program—God's Will in Our Lives

1. Robert Browning, "Rabbi ben Ezra", xxxii. *One Thousand Quotable Poems, An Anthology of Modern Verse*. Compiled by Thomas Curtis Clark and Esther Gillespie. (Willet, Clark, and Co.: Chicago and New York, 1937), 67.
2. Adelaide Pollard, "Have Thine Own Way, Lord." Stanza 1, in *Hymns for the Family of God,* ed. Fred Bock (Nashville, TN: Paragon Associates, Inc., 1976), 400.

FOUR
Strength in Our Weakness

1. Dr. Ole Hallesby, *Prayer* (London: InterVarsity Press, 1948), 13.
2. D.M. Lloyd-Jones, *The Final Perseverance of the Saints* (Edinburgh: The Banner of Truth Trust, 1975), 135-46.

FIVE
The Spirit of Faith

1. A.J. Gordon, *The Ministering of the Spirit* (Minneapolis, MN.: Bethany House Publishers, 1985), 12-13.

SIX
Abounding in Hope

1. Jurgen Moltmann, *The Theology of Hope* (London: SCM Press, 1967), 20.
2. James G. Small, "He Drew Me with Cords of Love," in *Hymns for the Family of God* (Nashville, Tenn.: Paragon Associates, Inc., 1976), 220.
3. James S. Stewart, *River of Life* (Nashville, TN.: Abingdon Press, 1972), 134.
4. Oscar Wilde, *The Ballad of the Reading Gaol*, III, 31.
5 Amy Carmichael, *Edges of His Ways* (Fort Washington, PA: Christian Literature Crusade, 1975), 144.

EIGHT
Overcoming Yesterday

1. H. Jackson Brown Jr., *Live and Learn and Pass It On* (Nashville, TN: Rutledge Hill Press, 1991, 1992). A number of short excerpts are included from this book in the text.
2. Author unknown.
3. *A Mind Awake: An Anthology of C.S. Lewis,* ed.by Clyde S. Kilby, (New York: Harcourt, Brace and World, 1968, 1969).
4. Based on the poem "Start Where You Stand: by Benton Braley, in *Poems that Touch the Heart,* compiled by A.L. Alexander (Garden City, N.Y.: 1956).

NINE
Ready for Battle: Discerning and Armed

1. Michael P. Green, *Illustrations for Biblical Preaching* (Grand Rapids, MI: Baker Book House, 1982), 383-84.
2. Henry Van Dyke, "With Eager Heart and Will on Fire," in public domain.

ELEVEN
Check the Dailies

1. This rewording is based on the last verse from a poem entitled "The
Secret" in the book, *Spiritual Hilltops* by Ralph Spaulding Cushman,
published by Abingdon Press. It has been reprinted recently in *Wings of
Joy* by Joan Winmill Brown (Old Tappan, NJ: Fleming H. Revell
Company, 1977), 45. The original verse by Cushman reads:

> So I think I know the secret
> Learned from many a troubled day:
> You must seek the Lord in the morning
> if you want Him through the day!

2. E.W. Blandy, from the hymn "Where He Leads Me," in *Hymns for the
Family of God* (Nashville, TN: Paragon Associates, Inc., 1976), 607.

About the Author

If you were to ask Lloyd Ogilvie what he does, his quick reply would be, "I'm a listener!" That may seem like an unusual response from a person who is known for his speaking and writing, but what Dr. Ogilvie has to say comes from attentive listening—to God and to people.

In addition to his pastoral counseling and extensive correspondence, each year he does a survey of what's on the minds and hearts of his congregation and his radio and television audiences. Then, in prayer and study, he listens to God for His answers in the Bible. This relational approach to communicating the Gospel has made his messages on-target biblical expositions addressing the deepest concerns and most urgent questions of people. He has dedicated his life to the "exciting adventure of discipleship," and to communicating his discoveries to others in a vivid, practical, down-to-earth way. He combines a rich blend of scholarship and fresh inspiration with real-life illustrations, anecdotes, and stories about the great adventure of life in Christ.

Dr. Ogilvie is the Senior Pastor of the historic First Presbyterian Church of Hollywood. His radio and television ministry, *Let God Love You*, is broadcast throughout the nation. In 1988, he was named "Preacher of the Year" by the National Association of Religious Broadcasters.

He is the author of thirty-five books in which his readers are brought into the very presence of Jesus Christ, where they can experience the love, compassion, and healing power of the Lord. Dr. Ogilvie also serves as the General Editor of the *Communicator's Commentary*, a thirty-five volume exposition of the books of the Bible, and is a contributor to many magazines. His speaking engagements take him to conferences and retreats throughout the world.

As pastor of his church, Dr. Ogilvie leads a large staff of pastors and professional workers in equipping the members of the church for their ministry in the world. The church is distinguished for its healing ministry and its many task-force groups working to impact the major social problems of the Los Angeles area.

Dr. Ogilvie was educated at Lake Forrest College, Garrett Theological Seminary, and New College, University of Edinburgh. He holds doctoral degrees from Witworth College, Redlands University, Moravian Seminary, and Eastern College.

Another Book to Help You Grow in the Spiritual Life

The Magnificent Vision
Seeing Yourself through the Eyes of Christ
Lloyd John Ogilvie

If you want to develop a fresh and deeper vision for your life, Lloyd Ogilvie can help. In *The Magnificent Vision* he points out that to be in Christ as believer, disciple, and as a loved and forgiven person is only half of the blessing God intends. The second half consists in having Christ in you as *motivator, enabler,* and *transformer of personality.*

The truth is that the Lord has a much more exciting vision for your life than you do. He wants you to be joyful, whole, and pure, just like himself. He wants to show you how to develop the fruit of the Holy Spirit in your life.

Lloyd Ogilvie knows that Christ longs to give us more of himself. In *The Magnificent Vision,* he takes a closer look at what it means to surrender to Christ so that we can grow in the fruit of the Holy Spirit and in greater intimacy with him. This book was originally published as *The Radiance of the Inner Splendor. $8.99*